Bit Part Players of the Bible

Over 100 lesser-known characters on God's stage

Bit Part Players of the Bible

Ray Markham

OTHER BOOKS BY RAY MARKHAM

What Kind of Power is This?
(on the miracles of Jesus)

Pointed and Personal
(on the parables of Jesus)

Greater Expectations
(on the Sermon on the Mount)

These three all published by Autumn House and come with questions for group study.

The Olympics of Life
(a thought-for-the-day book)

Keep Your Eye on the Ball
(a thought-for-the-day book)

These two both published by The Leprosy Mission International

---

Copyright © Ray Markham 2007

Published 2007 by CWR, Waverley Abbey House, Waverley Lane, Farnham, Surrey GU9 8EP, UK.
Registered Charity No. 294387. Registered Limited Company No. 1990308. Reprinted 2008.

See back of book for list of National Distributors.

Unless otherwise indicated, all Scripture references are from the Holy Bible: New International Version (NIV), copyright © 1973, 1978, 1984 by the International Bible Society.

Other Bible versions are marked:
AV: The Authorised Version
Phillips: J.B. Phillips, *The New Testament in Modern English*, © 1960, 1972, J.B. Phillips, Fount Paperbacks

Concept development, editing, design and production by CWR
Cover image: Stockxpert/Bluestock

Printed in Finland by WS Bookwell

ISBN: 978-1-85345-445-5

Contents

Other bit part players also making an appearance in the following chapters are:

2. Ishmael
3. Eliezer
4. Dinah, Simeon, Levi, Tamar, Benjamin
5. Othniel
6. Dathan, Abiram, On
9. Eglon
10. Barak, Sisera, Heber, Jael
11. Jephthah's daughter
12. Elimelech, Mahlon, Kilion, Orpah
13. Elkanah, Hophni, Phinehas
14. Ish-bosheth, Abner, Paltiel
15. Abner, Abishai, Asahel, Uriah, Nathan, Absalom, Amasa, Adonijah, Benaiah
16. Adoniram, Shemaiah, Shishak
17. Ahijah, Abijah
18. Azariah, Baasha, Hanani
19. Ahab, Athaliah, Micaiah, Zedekiah, Jehu, Jahaziel, Ahaziah
20. Shunammite woman, Naaman
21. Joram, Ahaziah, Jezebel, Jehonadab
22. Athaliah, Jehosheba, Jehoiada, Zechariah
23. Jehoash
24. Hezekiah, Amon
25. Hilkiah, Huldah, Nebuchadnezzar, Neco, Jehoiakim, Jehoiachin, Zedekiah
26. Nebuchadnezzar
27. Jeshua, Haggai, Zechariah

To all the 'bit part players' who have influenced my life without knowing it, including Nellie Sanderson, who touched a young boy's heart with her gripping accounts of the lives of many Old Testament characters.

Preface

The Old Testament is full of 'bit part players': people who play only a small part on the biblical stage, and are therefore often overlooked or not paid much attention to. In my opinion, this is a great pity, as there is much to be learnt from these people that is of relevance and help to our daily lives.

This book attempts to portray some of these characters in an interesting and exciting way that will also encourage and challenge us. Most of us could be described as 'bit part players', and it is my prayer that this book will stimulate us to play our parts to the full on the stage where God has placed us, for His honour and glory. After all, we never know whose life we may be influencing.

Chapter 1

Make it Easy on Yourself

Lot

Genesis 13:5–13; 14:1–16; 19:1–38

Growing up

Ur of the Chaldeans must have been an amazing place to live. It was one of the most important cities in the ancient world, and was the centre for worship of the moon god Sin, also known as Nannar. The city was full of imposing buildings, but dominating them all was a huge ziggurat, the tower of the temple dedicated to Sin. Ur was a flourishing centre of civilisation, with an enormous library. Situated on the river Euphrates in southern Iraq, Ur was also a large trading centre, and had a cosmopolitan atmosphere. The citizens of Ur led comfortable lives, and were well educated. It was into such a culture and environment that Lot was born.

His father's name was Haran, but nothing is known about his mother or what happened to her. Haran died when Lot was still young, which must have been very difficult for him to cope with. However, he was fortunate enough to have a caring family around

11

him, particularly his uncle, Abram, and his grandfather, Terah. Abram and his wife Sarai had no children at this time, so it seems that they took Lot under their wing. Lot grew up experiencing the love of a close-knit family, receiving the best education it was possible to have at the time, and living in very agreeable surroundings.

On the move

Following the call of God to Abram to leave Ur and 'go to the land I will show you' (Gen. 12:1), 'Terah took his son Abram, his grandson Lot son of Haran, and his daughter-in-law Sarai, the wife of his son Abram, and together they set out from Ur of the Chaldeans to go to Canaan. But when they came to Haran, they settled there' (11:31). It was only after Terah died, that Abram moved on from the city of Haran to the land of Canaan. 'He took his wife Sarai, his nephew Lot, all the possessions they had accumulated and the people they had acquired in Haran, and they set out for the land of Canaan, and they arrived there' (12:5).

What a cultural shock this must have been for all of them, including Lot. One minute he was living in a city, with all its comforts; the next minute he was living out in the countryside, with all its *dis*comforts. The city-dweller had become a nomadic tent-dweller; his lifestyle had changed dramatically.

Abram's family was not the only one moving across this productive land known as 'The Fertile Crescent' around the year 1900 BC. Many others were doing the same. But Abram's family was the only one making this journey in response to the call of the one true God. Did Abram explain the circumstances leading up to this massive step of faith he was taking to his nephew, now a young man? And what did Lot think of his uncle's decision? Obviously he had to accept it, whether he agreed with it or not, but either way he must have been impressed by Abram's faith in God, and his willingness to shoulder the consequences of such a faith.

In comparison to Abram's great faith in God, the faith of many of us may seem very small. But be encouraged! Jesus tells us that if we have faith as small as a mustard seed – the smallest seed of all – we can achieve great things for God (Matt. 17:20–21). Now that's really exciting, because it means that each one of us can play a part in the growth of God's kingdom. May God help us to trust Him wholly and obey Him completely (Prov. 3:5–6), to accept the implications of our belief in Him for the way we live our lives (Matt. 3:8), and to step out in faith at His command (Matt. 14:28–29).

The Egypt experience

Some years later, there was a famine in the land. Their only choice was to journey down south into the land of Egypt, where Abram became 'very wealthy in livestock and in silver and gold' (13:2), albeit due to deceiving the Pharaoh into thinking Sarai was his sister (12:11–20). Was this the first time that Lot saw his uncle afraid? Maybe it came as a relief to Lot that, although his uncle had great faith in God, he was still human, and prey to human failings.

In those times when we feel afraid, or do wrong things, isn't it encouraging to know that great men of faith like Abram felt and did exactly the same? And isn't it even more wonderful to see how God always brings blessing even out of the darkest times, as we submit ourselves and our circumstances to Him?

The upshot of this incident was that Abram and his household were expelled from Egypt. They went back to Canaan, and finally settled near Bethel.

The parting of the ways (Genesis 13:5–13)
It's your decision

It seems that by now Lot had become independent of Abram, though he was still part of his household. He was now at the stage of employing his own herdsmen to look after his own flocks. But there was a problem. Abram and Lot had become so successful in animal husbandry that the land couldn't support the grazing requirements of all the flocks and herds. It had got so bad that there had been a number of punch-ups between Abram's herdsmen and those employed by Lot. A parting of the ways was the only possible solution to the problem. As the older of the two, Abram had the right to choose which way he would go, leaving Lot to take the opposite direction; but surprisingly he gave Lot the choice: 'If you go to the left, I'll go to the right; if you go to the right, I'll go to the left' (13:9b).

Why did he allow Lot this privilege? Maybe he felt confident that wherever he went he would make a success of things. Perhaps it was another example of his supreme faith in God that whatever happened, the Lord would bless him. Maybe he asked God what he should do, and was being obedient. Or could it be that he knew very well where Lot would choose to go, and he preferred to go in the opposite direction anyway, so he could afford to be magnanimous?

Making the choice

I wonder what thoughts were uppermost in Lot's mind as he made the choice? He certainly doesn't seem to have consulted God about it, but rather acted according to his own selfish instincts and interests. 'Lot looked up and saw that the whole plain of the Jordan was well watered ... So Lot chose for himself the whole plain of Jordan' (vv.10–11). He was certainly taking the easier option with regard to his future prosperity in the animal business. Also, could it be that he had never fully adjusted to the nomadic lifestyle, and still yearned deep down for a return to the attractions of city life? Whatever the case, it probably didn't take him long to make up his mind. So, 'Lot lived among the cities of the plain and pitched his tents near Sodom' (v.12), thus bringing his preferred lifestyle within reach once again.

But, although it looked good, and it seemed right, and he was convinced it was for the best, he was making the wrong choice. 'Now the men of Sodom were wicked and were sinning greatly against the LORD' (v.13). Surely Lot must have heard about what was going on in Sodom before he made his decision? And yet he just pushed any thoughts of this to the back of his mind, preferring to make it easy on himself.

This incident shows a lot about Lot! He just wasn't prepared to make the tough choices. It was always the easy way out for him; he would always take the line of least resistance. He didn't anticipate or think through the consequences of his actions; he just lived for the present, and paid for it in the future. He wanted the best for himself, but he didn't count the cost.

It's easy to criticise Lot, but I wonder how often we are guilty of making difficult or important choices in a similar manner? If my experience is anything to go by, it's easy to fall into the trap of taking the selfish option, of being influenced by the wrong people or motives, of choosing the easy way out, of making a choice because it seems right or looks good, of not anticipating the consequences or counting the cost of our actions. It's easy to be guided by our own natural instincts rather than to commit everything to God in prayer, and be guided by the One who knows the end from the beginning.

Family matters

And what about Abram's role in all this? Should he have given the responsibility of making the choice to Lot in the first place? Shouldn't he have accepted his position as the elder and made the decision himself, as would have been proper? And, having saddled his nephew with such an important and life-changing choice, shouldn't Abram at least have discussed with Lot the dangers of moving in the direction of such a place as Sodom? True, Lot may well have dismissed such warnings and decided to go there anyway, in which case he couldn't turn round in the future and blame Abram for what subsequently occurred.

It seems to me that this incident raises some important

questions with regard to family life. For example, do we sometimes abrogate our responsibilities as parents and expect our children to make important decisions without giving them the benefit of our experience? Do we discuss family matters together and come to agreed conclusions, or do we just ignore tensions and hope they'll go away?

And what do we do when our children decide to go their own way, in spite of all our advice and even pleading? In this case, Abram provides us with an excellent example of how to react. As we shall see, Abram kept in contact with Lot, went and helped him out in difficult times, and beseeched God on his behalf. The easy way out for Abram would have been to wash his hands of Lot at their parting of the ways, but he didn't. I believe that he kept on loving him and praying for him through it all. Abram kept the lines of communication open between them, even though he must have despaired of Lot's behaviour at times. Like Abram, shouldn't we take the difficult option, and do the same? Isn't that what God would have us do?

Abram rescues Lot (Genesis 14:1-16)

Some time later, Lot and his family actually moved into the city of Sodom from the plains outside, and took up residence there (14:12). The magnetism of city life had obviously become too strong for him to resist.

In those days, most cities had a king, and Sodom was no exception. Along with other cities in the area, Sodom paid tribute money to Kedorlaomer, the king of Elam so he wouldn't come and trash the place. After twelve years of this, Bera, the king of Sodom, along with the kings of four other cities, had had enough, and rebelled by not paying their tribute. The reaction of Kedorlaomer was predictable enough: he and his allies came and ransacked the offending cities, including Sodom. Lot's family and possessions were carried off as part of their booty, and they faced possible torture, slavery and death. Despite the fact that they had parted company, Abram immediately went into action. At great personal risk, he and his 318 trained men rode to Lot's rescue, and routed the enemies of Sodom. 'He recovered all the goods and brought back his relative Lot and his possessions, together with the women and the other people' (v.16).

Imagine Abram's reaction then when Lot decided to go back to Sodom to live. Some people never learn, do they? And throughout his life, Lot seems to have been one such person. Many of us know exactly how Abram must have felt. There have been times when we too have put ourselves out for other people, only to feel let down by what they did next. For all those of us who have been in that situation, the question is: 'What do *we* do next?' The apostle Paul, who must have experienced such feelings many times during his life, wrote: 'Let us not become weary in doing good' (Gal. 6:9). When we are tempted to give up on people, it's good to remember that God never gives up on us.

Sodom destroyed (Genesis 19:1–29)
Abraham's visitors

Many years later, Abram, now called Abraham (17:5), had some angelic visitors (18:1–33). When he realised that they were on their way to destroy Sodom, he pleaded with them to spare those living in the city who were righteous. Obviously, he would have had Lot and his family in mind. However, Abraham came to realise that such people were very thin on the ground in Sodom, and there was no alternative for the city but to come under God's judgment.

Was Abraham tempted to go to Sodom and warn Lot to escape while he had the chance? Or did he think that his nephew wouldn't even listen to his advice any more? Besides which, he may have reasoned, Lot is old enough to make his choice and will have to live with the consequences of his decision. Or did he believe that, in His mercy, God would make a way of escape for Lot, and bring him out of that situation? Whether he did or not, Abraham must have prayed about the situation, because God heard his cry and answered it (19:29).

Many of us who are parents will have experienced the same agony of seeing our grown-up children make what we think is the wrong choice, and suffer the consequences. But there comes a time when we as parents have to let go, and allow our offspring to make their own mistakes. This isn't easy, especially as we often feel guilty and blame ourselves, quite wrongly in most cases. We can't change what has happened, but we can pray in faith that God will keep His hand upon them and bring them out of that situation. God heard Abraham's prayers, and He will hear ours too.

The prevailing culture

In those days, the gateway of a city was where the elders and leaders met to discuss community matters. It was a place of prestige and authority, and the city officials liked to be seen there. Since Lot 'was sitting in the gateway of the city' (v.1) when the angels arrived, it seems that he had become one of the leaders of Sodom. Ominously, he was there on his own, which suggests he had been ostracised by the other leaders, presumably because he disagreed with their lifestyle and way of doing things.

How could Lot, with the righteous upbringing that he had had, bear to live in such a city as Sodom, where homosexuality was rampant, let alone become one of its leaders? Did he think that if he got into a position of leadership he could change the culture of Sodom? Or had he become so comfortable with city life in Sodom that he found it easier to compromise with the prevailing culture, and ignore the wickedness around him, rather than try to fight against it? In his second letter, Peter says that Lot was 'a righteous man, who was distressed by the filthy lives of lawless men (for that righteous man, living among them day after day, was tormented in his righteous soul by the lawless deeds he saw and heard)' (2 Pet. 2:7–8). However, it seems that Lot had compromised with the lifestyle and mores of Sodom to the point that, when he did try to take a stand against the attitudes of the people, he was sneered at and not taken seriously (v.9).

Paul pleads with us 'Don't let the world around you squeeze you into its own mould' (Rom. 12:2, Phillips). It's not easy to keep on fighting against the prevailing culture: we can soon find ourselves being squeezed by it, sucked into it, and accepting it, rather than standing up for what is right in God's sight. May God give us the strength to stand together as His people and to keep on fighting tirelessly against all that is evil and wrong in our society.

The angels in Sodom

I wonder if the writer to the Hebrews had Lot in mind when he wrote: 'Do not forget to entertain strangers, for by so doing some people have entertained angels without knowing it' (Heb. 13:2)? Lot insisted that the strangers spent the night at his house rather than in the city centre as they proposed (vv.2–3).

Word of the strangers' arrival soon spread round the city, and Lot suddenly heard men's voices outside shouting for him to bring his visitors out 'so that we can have sex with them' (v.5). Lot went out to talk to them and, unbelievably, offered his two daughters to the men for sex, presumably out of sheer desperation to protect his guests (vv.6–8). Their sneering reply showed what they really thought of Lot, and they moved forward to break down the door (v.9).

Fortunately for Lot, the angels reached out and pulled him back inside the house and shut the door. They then struck the men outside with blindness so they couldn't find the door (vv.10–11). Was it at this point that Lot realised these visitors to the city were more than just men? He was certainly left in no doubt about this when they told him to gather his family together ready to get out of Sodom, because God had sent them to destroy the city (vv.12–13).

Interestingly, when Lot found his future sons-in-law and told them that 'the LORD is about to destroy the city', they 'thought he was joking' (v.14). How many times have we experienced the same sort of reaction from people when we try to tell them that God is not only a God of love and mercy, but of judgment, and that one day each one of us will have to give an account of our lives to him? How we need to pray that there might be a renewed sense of sin in our society, and a realisation that God in His mercy has sent Jesus to save us from our sin, just as He sent the angels to rescue Lot and save him from God's judgment on Sodom.

Because they didn't believe the message, Lot's sons-in-law died in the destruction that rained down on Sodom the next morning, while Lot, his wife and daughters escaped from the city at the urging of the angels (vv.15–25). God's mercy to Lot and his family shines through this story. Even when Lot hesitated to leave this sinful city that he had allowed to penetrate deeply into his soul, the angels 'grasped his hand and the hands of his wife and of his two daughters and led them safely out of the city, for the LORD was merciful to them' (v.16).

What a beautiful picture that scene conjures up in our minds, as God extends his hands of mercy towards them, takes hold of them, and brings them out to safety. How wonderfully it reminds us of God's mercy to us, as He reaches down with hands extended towards us, takes hold of us, and lifts us out of the slough of our sinfulness and brings us into the safety of His presence (see Psa. 40:1–3).

Lot's wife and daughters (Genesis 19:26,30–38)
It seems that Lot's wife was even more attached to Sodom than her husband was, because she couldn't help but stop and look back at what was happening to the city, in spite of being told expressly not to do so (19:17). As she lingered and gazed in horror at the scene before her, she was caught up in the destruction. Her demise is recorded in these chilling words: 'But Lot's wife looked back, and she became a pillar of salt' (v.26).

Jesus told us to 'Remember Lot's wife!' (Luke 17:32). Interestingly, the context of these words is also the coming of the judgment of God. Jesus was stressing how important it is to obey

His commands, and not to be distracted from following them by the things of the world. Disobedience to God always proves costly.

As for Lot's two daughters, their main concern was to bear children, as the culture of those days dictated. Now their prospective husbands were dead, and they were confined to the solitary life of the mountains, where were they to find men by whom to have offspring? They were desperate. The only man around was their father, so they contrived to have children by him.

What a tragic and pitiful state for Lot to find himself in: drunk and naked in a cave with his daughters. Perhaps if he had gone back to Abraham's household after the events in Sodom his daughters would have found husbands there; and this situation, which smacks of the morals of Sodom, might never have occurred.

As a result of these incestuous relationships, they each had a son. The older daughter named hers Moab, which sounds like the Hebrew for 'from father'; the younger called hers Ben-Ammi, which means 'son of my people'. Ironically, the descendants of Lot's grandsons, the Moabites and the Ammonites, became great enemies of Israel, the descendants of Abraham. They lived to the east of the River Jordan, and Israel never conquered them.

Lot's life serves as a warning against trying to make life easy for ourselves by compromising with the world around us; against refusing to make tough decisions in favour of taking the easy, more selfish option; and against failing to anticipate or appreciate the consequences of our actions. May God help us to avoid these pitfalls in our own lives.

Chapter 2

A Pawn in the Game

Hagar

Genesis 16:1–16; 21:1–21
(Other bit part player appearing: Ishmael)

Giving God a helping hand (Genesis 16:1–6)
God's promise

Soon after Abram rescued Lot and his family from King Kedorlaomer (see Chapter 1), God spoke to him. In spite of his triumphant victory, Abram was feeling very depressed, because he and Sarai still had no children. This meant that his estate would pass into the hands of Eliezer, one of his servants. But God reassured him that 'This man will not be your heir, but a son coming from your own body will be your heir' (Gen. 15:4). Abram believed God's promise (15:6) for many years, and held on to it in faith; but still nothing happened.

And this can be our experience too. God may promise us, quite clearly and distinctly, that something is going to happen in our lives: so we keep believing, we have faith, we hold on to that promise – and yet nothing seems to happen. In my experience, God's promises rarely come to pass immediately. It's usually over a period of time that things begin to work out, and we find God fulfilling what He has promised.

When doubt creeps in

The trouble was that, during this time of waiting, Abram and Sarai got to the point where they were beginning to doubt God's promise. If we're honest, many of us have also done the same. It's so easy to do, isn't it? Time goes by, and we keep on praying, and then after a while we find ourselves wondering whether anything is ever going to change, whether anything is ever going to happen; and that's when doubt creeps in.

So Sarai decided that she was going to give God a helping hand, by which she meant taking matters into her own hands; and Abram agreed to her plan (16:2). They tried to make God's promise come true in their way. But their impatience and impetuousness would prove to be disastrous, bringing in its wake problems for them personally, and also for their descendants, the nation of Israel.

Isn't this a danger that we all face – trying to make God's promise come to pass in the way that we think it should, even to the extent of giving God a helping hand, simply because we're getting impatient or doubt has crept in? Yet how often do we find in our experience that God doesn't do it in our way at all, because God has His own way of doing things, and His own time for doing things (Isa. 55:8–9)? In my experience, it is even possible to thwart God's purposes by doing this, thus delaying the fulfilment of the promise. Isn't it better to leave matters in the hands of the One who holds the whole world in His hands?

The surrogate mother

Sarai had a maidservant called Hagar, and she was to become a pawn in the game of inheritance. They had acquired her during their undistinguished yet profitable time in Egypt (Gen. 12:10–20). Although she was from Egypt, the name Hagar is not Egyptian, so it must have been given to her by Abram. 'Hagar' actually means 'flight' or 'runaway', which makes one wonder if she had tried to run away from Abram and Sarai to avoid having to leave Egypt with them. After all, who would fancy leaving their family and the settled comforts of Egypt for a nomadic lifestyle somewhere up north? So 'Hagar' became her name, and was to prove significant in her life.

Sarai seems to have come to the conclusion that God's promise to Abram was not going to be fulfilled through her: 'The LORD has kept me from having children' (v.2), she told her husband. So, through whom could the promise be fulfilled if not through her? The answer was standing right there in her tent. Hagar was the obvious surrogate mother.

This practice to ensure a male heir was quite legal in those times, as testified by tablets from places such as Nuzi and Ur of the Chaldeans, from where Abram and Sarai originated. Any child thus born to a slave girl was considered as the wife's own child, if she had no children of her own. This was the way things were done in the city they had come from.

God had brought them out of that culture into a new situation, and yet in this time of anxiety, what did they do? They went back to their old culture to try and find some answers there. Isn't it tempting when we are anxious about something, and God doesn't seem to be answering our prayers, to seek answers in the culture of the world we once lived by?

Sarai didn't check out her idea with God; and neither, incidentally, did Abram, who we always think of as doing the right thing. Sarai just assumed that as it was the obvious course of action it must be the right course of action. She would solve the problem herself, and in that way God's promise to Abram would come to pass.

As we all know, just because something seems obvious doesn't mean it's right. In my experience, it's easy to go away from God in times of doubt and seek the solution elsewhere; to act according to our own wisdom. But often that will only cause more problems, as it did for Abram and Sarai.

Two queens

Hagar, of course, had no choice in the matter. She was forced into a loveless marriage of convenience (v.3): at Sarai's convenience, and *for* Sarai's convenience! Hagar's thoughts and feelings were not taken into account. She might not even have liked Abram, yet she was forced to have sex with him. As a mere slave, she might well have expected such treatment, but still she must have found it rather hard to bear. The only joy she got was becoming pregnant (v.4). In those days, it was considered a disgrace for women not to bear children, as we see in the stories of Hannah and Elizabeth, for example (1 Sam. 1; Luke 1:25).

Now Hagar was pregnant by Abram, the dynamics of the situation had changed. No longer was it a case of a queen and a pawn; there were now two queens on the board! And that could only spell big trouble ahead for Abram; and so it proved. Hagar began to act arrogantly towards Sarai, and despised her openly. We can only imagine the words that passed between them, woman to woman, queen to queen: how Hagar would have taunted Sarai with the fact that she was pregnant and her mistress wasn't, and how Sarai would have responded to that. What a wonderful opportunity this was for Hagar to get her own back for being used by her mistress! Imagine Sarai's feelings as she looked at Hagar getting bigger every day, which just reinforced her own disgrace. Her state of mind must have been deteriorating day by day, as all these feelings become convoluted inside her.

Eventually enough was enough, as Sarai reached breaking point. And who did she blame for the situation? Why, Abram of course, even though it was all her idea! Imagine the scene between them as Sarai stormed in to give vent to her feelings – in a very loud voice. The tent must have been filled with the sound of her anger, and the whole camp could hear. They probably all stopped what they were doing to listen! Sarai, seething under the treatment dished out to her by her slave girl, turned her wrath on Abram: 'You are responsible for the wrong I'm suffering. I put my servant in your arms, and now that she knows that she is pregnant, she despises me. May the Lord judge between you and me' (v.5). So Sarai did partly admit her fault, but still held Abram responsible.

Abram, reeling under his wife's verbal attack, decided he'd be better off to keep well out of this situation, so he told Sarai to sort it out herself. '"Your servant is in your hands," Abram said. "Do with her whatever you think best"' (v.6). He didn't seem to think that he had a responsibility to sit down with his two wives, and calmly talk through the issues with them to resolve this awkward situation amicably. He just washed his hands of the situation, and left Sarai to deal with it in whatever way she chose. And Sarai did deal with it, in her own particular way. So there was spite for spite, as Sarai made her servant's life a complete and utter misery until Hagar could stand it no longer and, true to the name she was given, ran away.

While both women acted badly, Abram didn't act at all, with the result that he suddenly realised his pregnant wife had left the camp, and gone he knew not where. Presumably she was on her way back to Egypt, to the safety of her own people and her own culture.

Like Abram, are we guilty sometimes of not tackling issues within our families that need to be confronted and dealt with? Had he forgotten so soon the consequences of not dealing with the tensions caused between his herdsmen and Lot's? Like Sarai, do we blame other people for things that are clearly our own fault? And when given the opportunity to resolve conflicts, do we make them worse by being spiteful, or better by being gracious? Like Hagar, do we tend to run away from the problems that occur in our lives, or do we face up to them with courage and determination?

It's not easy to follow God; difficulties will arise. Sometimes things will go 'pear-shaped', as they did here. Isn't that the time to sort it out with God, and with the people involved, rather than what might appear to be the more attractive proposition of running away from the problem? And isn't it true that we learn more about God and grow more in God as we face up to things rather than take off at high speed in the opposite direction?

An angelic experience (Genesis 16:7-16)
Make a 'U' turn

On her way back to Egypt, an angel of the Lord appeared to this lonely, miserable, desperate runaway as she stopped to take a drink from a spring near the road (16:7). It's interesting that it is to Hagar that the angel appears: not to Abram, nor to Sarai, but to the one who is most bruised and needy. Does this not speak to us of the grace and mercy of God, who comes to us right where we are in our distress, no matter what we have done? Isn't it wonderful to know that God never forsakes us or abandons us, even when we are not where we should be?

Having come to her, and got her to admit the reality of her situation (v.8), what did the angel then tell Hagar to do about it (v.9)? Graciously, God had intervened in Hagar's life to stop her making another mistake. The angel told her to do two things: to return, and to submit. She was to go back and face up to what had happened. The solution was not in Egypt; the solution lay back where she came from. She needed to make a 'U' turn. God stopped the runaway because her return was going to get the problem dealt with, not just for Hagar herself, but for Abram and Sarai as well. And when she got there, she was to submit to Sarai, her mistress; and that was going to be really difficult for her. However justified she felt in her feelings towards Sarai, Hagar's attitude to her mistress was going to have to change.

Do we need to make a 'U' turn and face up to certain problems and difficulties that we have been running away from, maybe for years? Is there someone we have the wrong attitude towards, however justified we may feel in our stance, with whom we need to be reconciled (Matt. 5:24; Mark 11:25)? Do we need to submit to God and accept where He has placed us, whether we like it or not? God has actually put us there for a reason, and will use us for His glory there as we remain true to Him, even when things seem to go wrong. Both return and submission are crucial to having our joy and peace restored, as we see well illustrated in the parable of the prodigal (or lost) son (Luke 15:11–32).

Two promises

Having given Hagar two commands, the angel then gave her two promises (vv.10–11): everything would work out well for her; and she would be blessed through her son, who would have many descendants. The angel certainly didn't spare Hagar's feelings when he described the sort of cantankerous character her son would turn out to be (v.12). She was to name him 'Ishmael', which means 'God hears', a lovely reminder to Hagar that she was just as important as anyone else in God's sight, and He would always hear her when she cried out to Him.

Isn't it encouraging for us to know that when we return and submit, God's promises to us are just the same? He will bless us and work things out; He's always there and will hear our cry.

Over-well-med

It seems to me that Hagar was overwhelmed by God's loving care for her, particularly after the way she had behaved. As a memorial to this supernatural experience, she named the well where the angel found her 'well of the Living One who sees me' (vv.13–14, NIV footnote). She had experienced the living God speaking to her, and dealing with her. She responded with praise, gratitude, and probably tears of joy at the realisation that God's eyes were upon even her, a runaway slave girl. Isn't it amazing to think that the Almighty Creator God sees, knows and cares for each one of us, no matter how insignificant we may feel (Psa. 8:3–4)?

Return and submission

It must have taken a lot of courage for Hagar to return and submit. What sort of welcome would she get from Sarai? It would have been a lot easier for her to have been disobedient and to carry on down into Egypt: but then she would have lost God's blessing, joy and peace in her life. And isn't it the case that when we are disobedient to God, that's exactly what happens in our lives?

By the time Hagar arrived back at the camp in fear and trepidation, it seems that Sarai had calmed down; had she come to realise how wrong her treatment of Hagar had been? Hagar submitted, and returned to the role of pawn, with Sarai the undisputed queen. Hagar remained faithful to God by staying in the camp, and by naming her son 'Ishmael', in obedience to what the angel had said (vv.15–16). In fact, it was Abram who actually named the boy, so Hagar must have told him all about her angelic experience by the well. How thrilled Abram must have been to hear about these events, and how grateful he must have been to God for His intervention in the life of Hagar, thus allowing him the joy of seeing his son, which otherwise would have been denied him.

The birth and the feast (Genesis 21:1–14)
Thirteen years later

Thirteen years later, and there was still no sign of the promised son (17:1). Suddenly, God appeared to Abram, and confirmed His original promise (17:16). Was it their original doubt that was causing this long delay in the fulfilment of the promise? Whatever the reason, God made it clear this time that Sarai was to be the mother, so they didn't repeat their mistake. God also changed their names from Abram and Sarai to the more familiar Abraham and Sarah as a token of this renewed promise.

God kept faith with them, despite their failings. He could easily have abandoned them and chosen another couple to be the parents of His chosen people, but He didn't. Nor does God turn His back on us, or give up on us, when we let Him down. His mercy, forgiveness and love are unfailing. But, if we do decide to go our own way rather than God's, then it will always take time for God to bring us back to the way we should have been walking, so that His purposes can once again begin to be fulfilled in our lives. Yet the grace of God is such that, while we are going on our own little diversion, He never leaves us, but teaches us and causes us to grow through the mistakes we have made.

Interestingly, Abraham still had his doubts about God's promise. He even laughed and muttered to himself – but not to God! –

about the physical impossibility of it ever being fulfilled (17:17). He pleaded with God to bestow his blessing upon Ishmael, whom he obviously loved, but was told that, although Ishmael would be blessed, the covenant belonged to Isaac (17:18–22). The promise would be fulfilled in God's own time, so that everyone would have to acknowledge that the only possible explanation was that God had been at work (21:1–7).

Isn't it difficult to wait for God's timing to arrive? Isn't it hard to be patient, and keep on praying over the years about those situations we would rather like to see resolved right now? These events encourage us to do that, and remind us that God is faithful to His promises. They will come to pass in His time, and God will bring glory to Himself in that situation.

Don't laugh!

Interestingly, the name 'Isaac', given by God, means 'he laughs'. For me, this is a wonderful example of God's sense of humour! Whenever they used their son's name, Abraham and Sarah would have been reminded of the fact that they laughed when told of the prospective birth of Isaac (17:17; 18:12). It also serves as a reminder to us that God laughs at impossibilities, and delights to confound the wisdom of the world (Luke 1:37).

Abraham and Sarah both laughed at the promise of God. And aren't there times when God promises us something personally, or as a church, and we laugh, because we think it's just not possible? We think that God is bound to do it the 'Ishmael way', the way that is part of our experience already, the way that we know. But wait! Perhaps God wants to introduce something completely different into our lives, into our church. Perhaps God wants to do it the 'Isaac way', and take us down paths we've never trod before, giving us experiences we've never had before, seeing God work in ways we've never known before.

The day of the feast

Two to three years after the birth of Isaac, Abraham held a great feast to celebrate the fact that the child was now weaned. Who would have thought that such a happy occasion would be the setting for such distress? The restored tranquillity of the household was about to be shattered once again.

It all started when 'Sarah saw that the son whom Hagar the Egyptian had borne to Abraham was mocking' (v.9). Interestingly, the name 'Ishmael' is not used in this verse, or indeed in the whole account given of this incident. Was this done to emphasise the fact that Isaac was now all-important, and Ishmael of no importance?

What did Ishmael, now about fifteen years old, actually do that upset Sarah so much, and caused her to react so forcefully? It's not very clear at all. The word translated 'mocking' literally means 'isaacing', or 'laughing'. So Ishmael was apparently isaacing Isaac! Was he just playing about and being stupid, like any teenager might do? Or was he going out of his way to make fun of Isaac at every possible opportunity? Was he actually being disdainful of Isaac as Abraham's heir, maybe to the point of letting it be known that he considered himself as Abraham's rightful heir, being the eldest, and not this recently arrived half-brother of his?

Whichever it was, Sarah was furious. She saw Ishmael as a threat to Isaac's inheritance, and insisted that Abraham remove the boy and his mother from the camp permanently (v.10). Unlike that similar occasion thirteen years previously, Abraham decided that he must act. The word translated 'distressed' (v.11) actually means 'exploded in anger'. That the situation caused such a violent reaction within him is completely understandable. Abraham knew that, according to the law of the time, driving them out would mean Ishmael would be disinherited, which was actually prohibited by the customs of the day. So he was being backed into a legal corner here. But it wasn't just an issue of law. It was an issue of love. He loved Ishmael, his son, and he didn't want to lose him. What loving father could ever bring himself to drive his son away for ever? What a dilemma to be in! He must have been in turmoil both mentally and emotionally.

The cost of obedience

But God graciously spoke words of comfort and encouragement into Abraham's breaking heart, making it clear what he must do: 'Do not be so distressed about the boy and your maidservant. Listen to whatever Sarah tells you, because it is through Isaac that your offspring will be reckoned. I will make the son of the maidservant into a nation also, because he is your offspring' (vv.12–13).

What was Abraham's response? He had the courage to obey God, in spite of the cost: flouting the legal practice of the day would have cost him respect; losing his eldest son for ever would have cost him a broken heart. But Abraham had learnt that to obey God was the most important thing in life.

Abraham acted immediately in response to God's command. He almost seems to act with indecent haste. Maybe it was because he couldn't bear to postpone the pain of the moment any longer than necessary, because he knew it had to be done, and he just wanted to get on with it. So daybreak the very next day was witness to an extremely poignant scene (v.14), as Abraham personally put skins of food and water on to Hagar's shoulders, and said his goodbyes, no doubt embracing them both, with tears running down his cheeks. Sarah, quite probably, was nowhere to be seen.

And isn't it true that in order to obey God, we, like Abraham, have to learn to 'let go'? In my experience, we are sometimes called to 'let go' of things that are precious to us in order to be obedient to God, and that costs us; it may even cause us distress, cause us to question, cause us to wonder why. And when this happens, do we actually obey, or do we try to get round God's command, or accommodate it in some way? Do we sometimes hang on to the 'Ishmaels', which are precious to us, and lose the 'Isaacs', which are the things God really wants us to have, and which will bring us far more blessing and fulfilment that all the 'Ishmaels' put together ever could?

Back in the desert (Genesis 21:15-21)
Promise and provision

Once again, Hagar found herself in a desert place, but there are many contrasts between this time and the previous occasion. This time, 'the pawn' was there through no fault of her own. She wasn't running away: she had been sent away, and now she and her son were about to die on their way back to Egypt (vv.15–16). This time the angel called from heaven rather than appearing on earth; and he didn't ask her to do something as previously, but rather did something for her and her son, whose cry of distress had been heard by God (v.17). God heard the cry of 'God hears' (Ishmael), and opened the eyes of Hagar to see His provision of water for them (v.19). In this lovely way, God was showing that He is faithful to His promise: He promised Abraham that He would look after Ishmael, and here He was doing exactly that. God also made sure that Hagar knew He would be faithful to His promise concerning her offspring by repeating it (v.18).

Just as God provided water to meet Hagar's physical needs, so He has provided Jesus, the living water, to meet all our spiritual needs. As He explained, at another well to another woman who had been cast out: 'Everyone who drinks this water will be thirsty again, but whoever drinks the water I give him will never thirst. Indeed, the water I give him will become in him a spring of water welling up to eternal life' (John 4:13–14).

God continued to bless Ishmael, as He had promised Abraham He would (v.20). Nevertheless, the seeds of enmity had been sown, and the prophecy given to Hagar about her son (16:12) came to pass through him and his descendants (25:18). They became the Arab nations, who have always warred against each other, but are still united in their hatred of the descendants of Isaac – the Jews. A more salutary lesson about doing things God's way would be hard to find.

A symbol

Hagar is mentioned in Galatians 4:21–31. Paul uses Hagar, the slave woman, as a symbol of those who were slaves to the law, thinking it to be the way of salvation. By contrast he uses Sarah, the free woman, and her son Isaac as symbols of those who have come to faith in Christ, have been saved by grace and set free from their sin, as God promised. Like Isaac, we are children of God's promise.

Chapter 3

The Crafty Controller

Laban

Genesis 24:29–61; 29:1–30; 30:25–31:55
(Other bit part player appearing: Eliezer)

Opportunity knocks (Genesis 24:29–61)
Eliezer's arrival

When Abram left Haran to journey into the land of Canaan (see Chapter 1), his brother Nahor stayed behind. Nahor had a son named Bethuel, among whose children were Laban and Rebekah. Many years later, Abram, now called Abraham, sent his trusted servant Eliezer back to Haran to find a wife for his son Isaac from among his own people.

Eliezer met Rebekah as she came to draw water from the well where he had stopped, and he soon realised that this young lady was the answer to his prayers (24:12–21). When Eliezer explained to Rebekah who he was and why he had come, she ran back home in great excitement, and breathlessly told her family all that had occurred (vv.22–28).

Expensive gear

Laban noticed that his sister was now wearing some rather expensive gear: a gold nose ring, and two gold bracelets. He immediately sensed that there was a situation to be exploited here. So, with his eye to the main chance in sharp focus, and his greedy instincts working overtime, Laban wasted no time in rushing off to the well to ingratiate himself with the source of this obvious wealth. '"Come, you who are blessed by the LORD," he said', his voice dripping with spiritual veneer. '"Why are you standing out here? I have prepared the house and a place for the camels"' (v.31).

What a smoothie! We can almost see the insincerity in the false, flashing smile, and feel the greasiness oozing out of the hand proffered in welcome. Laban sent the servants into a flat spin stabling the camels, bringing water for feet-washing, and setting the best of food in large quantities before Eliezer and his men. Laban was determined to make the right impression in order to serve his self-centred motives.

Negotiations

As he heard about the vast wealth of Eliezer's master, and his quest to find a wife for Isaac from within Abraham's extended family, Laban must have found it difficult to contain himself. He must have been thinking, 'There's a lot of money to be made in this. All it needs is some careful negotiating!' Laban was in his favourite place: in control of the situation. The family didn't have to let Rebekah go, but clearly from Laban's perspective it was a situation to be exploited for his own gain. Indeed, it seems to have been Laban rather than Bethuel, his father, who took the lead in expediting matters, and Laban received 'costly gifts' (v.53) for his trouble.

It could also be said that Laban seems to have reacted with almost indecent haste in agreeing so quickly to the marriage: 'Here is Rebekah; take her and go' (v.51). Maybe Laban realised this when he'd slept on it, and that's why he tried to stall proceedings the next morning (v.55). However, Eliezer was keen to return to Abraham, and demanded that the matter be settled then and there. Rebekah agreed to go with Eliezer and become Isaac's wife, so the family blessed her, and said their fond farewells (vv.56–61).

Did Laban really see God's hand in all this (v.50), or was he just pretending to be spiritual in front of Eliezer to exploit the situation and get what he wanted? In my experience, we can often be tempted into being hypocritical at times as a means of getting what we want. The Pharisees' lives were characterised by hypocrisy: evidence of their self-centred motives. Didn't Jesus warn us not to be like them, but rather to live lives of integrity and truth (Matt. 5:37; 6:1–18; John 4:24)?

Jacob's arrival (Genesis 29:1–14)
Well, well

About forty years later, Rebekah's son Jacob was on the run from the wrath of his brother Esau, having deceived his father Isaac into bestowing the birthright upon him rather than upon his older twin brother (Gen. 27). Rebekah, who had orchestrated these proceedings, urged her favourite son to escape to Haran and take refuge with her brother Laban. Jacob needed no second bidding, and set off immediately. The fact that Jacob, very much his mother's son, and Laban were like two peas in a pod was going to make for some very interesting situations in the future.

Like Eliezer before him, Jacob came to a well. It was at a well that Eliezer had first seen Rebekah, whom Isaac would marry; and it was at a well that Jacob would first meet Rachel, Laban's younger daughter, whom he would marry. When Rachel came to the well, Jacob watered the sheep for her, and then told her who he was. Rachel ran off to tell her father Laban, who hurried out to meet Jacob. Laban welcomed Jacob with open arms, and took him home. Jacob then recounted to his uncle all the events that had brought him there. Having heard of all the devious goings-on involving his sister Rebekah and Jacob, it seems highly appropriate that Laban then said to Jacob, 'You are my own flesh and blood' (v.14).

How to use your daughters (Genesis 29:14–30)
Love her while you work

It can't have been long before Laban noticed that Jacob had fallen passionately in love with Rachel. He must have known that soon Jacob would be asking him for his daughter's hand in marriage. Characteristically, Laban decided to exploit Jacob's love for Rachel for his own benefit. Being in complete control of this situation, he could use it to maximum effect; and he did so in a very crafty way.

It seems Jacob was already proving himself to be a very valuable worker, and Laban wanted to keep it that way. In those days, a suitor would present the girl's family with a substantial gift, known as a dowry, by way of compensation for taking her away from them. Laban knew that, unlike Eliezer, Jacob had come with no material wealth to offer as a dowry; but he did have one valuable commodity that would do equally as well, and would greatly enhance Laban's own material prospects – his labour. He needed to tie Jacob down for as many years as possible so he couldn't strike out on his own. Also, Laban realised that his elder daughter, Leah, was not particularly attractive to men, but he really needed to get her married off. With a bit of craft and guile, he reckoned he could kill two birds with one stone.

Laban adopted a very reasonable and caring pose as he broached the subject of wages with Jacob (v.15). As Laban had anticipated, Jacob wanted his wages to constitute his dowry for Rachel, and he suggested to Laban that seven years' work would provide an acceptable amount (v.18). Laban seems to have been quite content with Jacob's suggestion, and pronounced himself happy that Rachel should marry within the family rather than outside it (v.19). 'So Jacob served seven years to get Rachel, but they seemed like only a few days to him because of his love for her' (v.20). How romantic! But, as Jacob was to discover, the course of true love never did 'run smooth'.

The deceiver deceived

Not surprisingly, when the seven years were completed, Jacob was somewhat impatient for the marriage to take place (v.21). So Laban organised the customary seven days of feasting to celebrate the marriage. On the first night, the bride, wearing a thick veil, would be brought to her husband.

How was it that Jacob didn't realise that he had been tricked; that the woman in his bed wasn't Rachel but Leah? Presumably the veil, the darkness and the alcohol had something to do with it. But whatever the reason, it was only when he woke up that Jacob became aware that he had been duped. As the Genesis account so delightfully puts it: 'When morning came, there was Leah!' (v.25). One can only imagine the look on Jacob's face as he turned over and saw Leah, not Rachel, lying there next to him.

Jacob must have been incandescent with rage as he stormed over to where Laban was, probably still wearing his night-clothes, and demanded an explanation. The deceiver was not best pleased at being deceived. In my experience, this can be true for us too. How often have we been angry about injustices done to us, yet been blasé about those we have done to others?

Seven years more

Now Jacob knew how Esau felt; his sin had come back to haunt him. But, whereas Jacob's deception could not be got around, Laban's subterfuge could, as his uncle smoothly pointed out to him. Craftily, Laban had omitted to inform Jacob that, in this part of the world, it was the custom that older daughters had to be married off before younger daughters could be. Because he had married Leah, Laban helpfully pointed out, he could now marry Rachel as well – but it would cost him another seven years' labour (vv.26–27).

The way Laban put it almost made it sound like he'd actually done Jacob a favour by his trickery. Laban must have been well-practised in the art of making deception and exploitation sound justifiable. Laban's utter selfishness is shown by the fact that he shamelessly exploited and used even his very own daughters to achieve his goals – a fact that they never forgot, and which would have consequences for him in the future.

Are we in danger of storing up trouble for ourselves in the future by our selfish attitudes, and by the self-centred decisions we are now making? Are other people, even those whom we love, suffering because of what we are doing? Doesn't being in control in a situation bring with it great responsibility to act in a way that does not exploit others for our own advantage, and does not stem from selfish motives? It's challenging to ask ourselves whether God would approve of the attitude we're taking, or the decision we're making. The psalmist was prepared to allow God to examine his heart (Psa. 139:23–24). Are we?

Poor old Jacob was in no position to argue; his uncle held the whip hand, so he had to submit meekly (v.28). To his credit, Jacob kept his side of the bargain, even though thoughts of getting even with his uncle must have crossed his mind. The time for that lay ahead. At the end of the week's celebrations, he married Rachel, 'And he worked for Laban another seven years' (v.30).

Outwitted (Genesis 30:25–31:21)
The sheep and the goats
After many years of barrenness, Rachel gave birth to Joseph. It was this event which prompted Jacob to ask Laban's permission to return to his homeland (30:25–26). Laban's reply had the veneer of religion about it, as he claimed that his idols had revealed that his increasing prosperity had been down to Jacob's presence and work for him (v.27). While not prepared to let him leave, Laban was prepared to retain Jacob on any terms his nephew cared to name (v.28). So Jacob made a proposal which seemed on the surface to give Laban the best of the deal (30:31–33).

Sheep were usually white, and goats were normally black. Jacob proposed that Laban should take away all the bicoloured animals and keep them for himself, leaving him with just the white and black ones. While the white sheep and the black goats would remain Laban's property, any bicoloured offspring of these animals would become Jacob's property: they would be his wages.

Laban would have considered that the chances of white sheep producing bicoloured lambs, and black goats giving birth to bicoloured kids to be extremely unlikely, so he agreed to Jacob's proposal and acted upon it immediately, lest his nephew should change his mind (vv.34–36).

Jacob, now well experienced in livestock management, had clearly worked out a system of selective breeding by which this seemingly unlikely outcome could be achieved. Exactly how the method described worked is not clear (vv.37–43) but, on Jacob's own admission (31:9), it was only successful because God's hand was at work in the process. The result was that 'the weak animals went to Laban and the strong ones to Jacob. In this way the man grew exceedingly prosperous and came to own large flocks, and maidservants and menservants, and camels and donkeys' (30:42–43).

Jacob had outwitted Laban by his cunning scheme. Laban the crafty controller had himself been craftily controlled. The exploiter had been exploited – and he didn't like it one bit, as described in these understated words: 'And Jacob noticed that Laban's attitude towards him was not what it had been' (31:2)! Laban must have been absolutely choked by Jacob's success. His sons were certainly angry and jealous at Jacob's wealth, which they reckoned Jacob had accrued over the last six years by taking advantage of their father (v.1). The situation was getting nasty; a storm was definitely brewing.

Even though Jacob was badly treated by Laban, God still caused him to prosper. Isn't it encouraging to know that God's power to bless us and to meet our needs is not limited by the way others might treat us or think of us?

Let's get out of here!

It was at this point that God spoke into the situation, and told Jacob to return home, with the promise that 'I will be with you' (v.3). Isn't it good to know that, whatever situation we are in, however unpleasant or difficult it may be for us, God has promised to be right there with us (Matt. 28:20; Heb. 13:5b–6)? Like Jacob, there are certain times in our lives when we particularly need to be reminded of that, so we can move forward with confidence.

So Jacob had a private conference with his wives Leah and Rachel out in the fields where they couldn't be overheard, and told them openly how he was feeling (vv.4–13). It was going to be far more difficult for him to escape from Laban than it had been to escape from Esau. He was part of Laban's household, and now had four wives and thirteen children, not to mention large flocks and herds. He would need the full support and help of Leah and Rachel to enable him to do this. Would they be prepared to leave their father and go with him to settle in a land that was foreign to them?

He needn't have worried. Leah and Rachel were still bristling over the shabby way Laban had treated them with regard to the dowry. The custom was that the daughters should receive the benefits of the dowry which was paid for them: in this case, fourteen years of labour which had brought Laban wealth. But he had blatantly failed to treat them properly in this matter. As they said, 'Not only has he sold us, but he has used up what was paid for us. Surely all the wealth that God took away from our father belongs to us and our children. So do whatever God has told you' (vv.15–16).

Thus encouraged, Jacob decided that now was the time to make a break for it. Laban was away shearing his sheep, which would give him three days start. For some reason that isn't clear, Rachel decided to steal Laban's household gods. Such idols were known as 'teraphim'. It was believed that they protected the home and provided advice. Legally speaking, the person who possessed them had inheritance rights. Small wonder that Laban was somewhat exercised over their disappearance (v.30)! Was Rachel afraid that Laban would consult these idols to find out where they had gone? Was she intending to claim the family inheritance? Or, as seems most likely, did she simply think the teraphim would give them all protection on their journey?

In pursuit (Genesis 31:22-55)
Laban's dream

When news of their flight reached Laban, he was so angry that he pursued Jacob, and finally caught up with him after a week's journey. As far as Laban was concerned, Jacob had gone off with what rightfully belonged to him. The scene was set for a furious confrontation, but God intervened, rebuking Laban and warning him to be careful about what he said and did (vv.24,42).

As a result of his dream, Laban appears to have changed his attitude completely. Instead of being angry and vengeful, which would have been in keeping with his character, Laban adopted the pose of the injured father and grandfather, who would have responded to any request to leave by giving them a really good send-off, which he was most upset had been denied him. He made it clear that he did not appreciate all this furtive underhandedness and deception; it could really all have been managed so much better if it had been done properly.

As far as Laban was concerned, he was always in the right, and was skilled at presenting himself in that light, whatever the truth may have been. Are we sometimes guilty of that too: never admitting we are wrong, thus avoiding having to face up to the wrong things we have done? Isn't it better to admit our own selfishness, which Laban could never bring himself to do, and put things right in a fair and just way?

Even though Laban was making out that he was in a conciliatory mood, he couldn't resist reminding Jacob who was actually in control of the situation; and that the only reason Jacob wasn't suffering at his hands was because of the intervention of 'the God of your father', whom Laban realised was too strong for him to stand against (v.29).

Head to head

But Laban was certainly not going to be conciliatory about his missing idols, and instituted a thorough search of all the tents, baggage and belongings. Rachel was actually sitting on them, and refused to get up on the grounds that she was having her period (v.35). So the teraphim remained undiscovered.

A head-to-head then took place between the two deceivers. An angry Jacob stood up to Laban. He listed all his grievances with him over the past twenty years; he maintained that if he had asked permission to leave, Laban would have sent him away with nothing; and he ended up with how God had vindicated him for his faithfulness of service to Laban in extremely adverse circumstances, while rebuking Laban for his selfish attitude (vv.36–42).

Like Jacob, are we faithful in service, even when we find what God has called us to do difficult? God has given each one of us a role to play in the work of His kingdom, and will empower us to carry it out as we put our trust in Him. Can God rely on us to see through to the end the task He has given us? Will He be able to say to us when we see Him face to face, 'Well done, good and faithful servant' (Matt. 25:21,23)?

Covenant

Laban doesn't seem to have been particularly moved by Jacob's heartfelt speech, and maintained that everything Jacob possessed actually belonged to him as head of the clan (v.43). However, Laban was pragmatic enough to realise that in opposing Jacob he was actually opposing God: a situation where he couldn't possibly win. Realising this, Laban knew he would have to compromise. So he proposed that they should make a covenant of peace, which was duly witnessed and celebrated by both sides (vv.44–55). Shortly after that, Laban and his men returned to Haran, while

Jacob journeyed on to Canaan.

As Jacob's camp disappeared over the horizon, did Laban shed a tear for what he had lost? His selfish, controlling attitude had cost him dear; his daughters and their children had gone, presumably never to be seen by him again. Did he even care? Did he change as a result of what had happened, or did he just carry on seeking to control, exploit and manipulate people for his own selfish ends?

Do we allow the experiences we go through to change us for the better? Or do we just carry on as if they'd never happened, wasting the potential they have for God to use them to make us more like Christ (2 Cor. 3:18)?

As for Jacob, he may have escaped from his uncle Laban; but going back home meant he would have to face Esau, the twin brother he had deceived all those years ago.

Chapter 4

Man of Water, Man of Action

Reuben and Judah

Genesis 34; 37; 38; 42–45; 49:3–4,8–12
(Other bit part players appearing: Dinah,
Simeon, Levi, Tamar, Benjamin)

Pen portraits
Reuben

Reuben was the first of Leah's six sons, and was clearly devoted to his mother (Gen. 30:14). His name means 'he has seen my misery' (29:32), since Leah believed Reuben was born because God had seen that she was not loved. Reuben was the firstborn of Jacob's twelve sons, and therefore enjoyed all the privileges of being in that position. These included a double portion of the family inheritance, and the honour of becoming leader of the family in due course.

But it would soon become clear that Reuben was just not leadership material. On his deathbed, his father Jacob described Reuben as being like water (49:4, AV), which has no form of its own, and shapes itself to fit its environment. As we shall see, Reuben was full of good intentions, but didn't have the courage to deliver. He tended to give in to group pressure and went along with the crowd, allowing them to shape him, and causing him to compromise his own convictions. Reuben had his own private values, but tended to contradict them by the way he acted in public. This made him untrustworthy, and he showed a lack of integrity at times. Reuben cut a sorrowful figure, because he tried so hard to do what was right, but was weak-willed and struggled to carry it through.

Judah

Judah, on the other hand, was just a natural-born leader. The fourth son of Leah, his name is derived from the Hebrew word for 'praise' (29:35). As we shall see, Judah was by no means perfect, but all Jacob's sons followed him readily, and looked to him for leadership rather than to Reuben. He was clear-thinking and decisive, if somewhat outspoken at times.

However, although Judah could be relied upon to take action, he made some awful decisions, mainly because he was influenced by the needs of the moment rather than anything else. But at least he was prepared to admit his mistakes and to take his share of the blame when confronted with what he had done.

Don't mess with us! (Genesis 34)
Dinah defiled

After their father Jacob's reconciliation with his brother Esau (32:3–21; 33:1–17), they moved on and camped outside the city of Shechem on a plot of land bought by Jacob from the sons of Hamor (33:19). Their sister, Dinah, decided to become part of the city's social scene, and soon attracted the attention of a man named Shechem, the son of Hamor. Although he had apparently fallen in love with Dinah, he couldn't wait to do things properly, and finished up raping her (vv.2–4).

Sexual passion caused problems then and it still causes problems today. Unless such deep feelings are controlled, they will have disastrous consequences – and not just for the two involved, but also for their families. No wonder Jesus spoke so strongly and so dramatically on the subject, telling us to take drastic action with ourselves if we find exercising strict self-control difficult (Matt. 5:27–30).

Dinah avenged

When Jacob's sons got to hear what Shechem had done, 'They were filled with grief and fury' (34:7). It seems they were appalled by their father's lack of action on the matter, and by the fact that Jacob was seemingly prepared to enter into marriage negotiations with Hamor and Shechem, so the brothers decided to take matters into their own hands. Meanwhile Dinah was in Shechem's house; whether or not by her own choice is unclear.

It should have been Reuben who spoke up on their behalf, as he was the firstborn, but more likely it was Judah. Because of Shechem's wicked deed, the brothers had no compunction about being deceitful in return. Hamor and Shechem were told that Jacob's family would go along with their proposals on one condition: that all their males be circumcised (vv.13–17).

Fuelled by the thought of getting their hands on Jacob's obvious wealth, the men of the city agreed, and were all circumcised (vv.18–24). 'Three days later, while all of them were still in pain, two of Jacob's sons, Simeon and Levi, Dinah's brothers, took their swords and attacked the unsuspecting city, killing every male' (v.25), and that included Hamor and his son. They took Dinah from Shechem's house, and went back to their camp (v.26).

Why didn't Reuben and Judah go on this killing spree with their brothers, Simeon and Levi? After all, they were Dinah's brothers too. We might have expected Reuben to chicken out, but surely not Judah. Maybe the two of them did not agree with the action proposed by Simeon and Levi, but they don't seem to have made much effort to restrain their brothers. In the end, all Jacob's sons were involved in plundering the city, seizing the dead men's animals, and carrying off their wealth and families (vv.27–29).

Jacob's criticism

Jacob took Simeon and Levi to task for what they had done, not because what they had done was immoral, but because their actions had put him, his household and his possessions in danger (v.30). Jacob was more concerned about saving his own skin than anything else!

Their justification for what they had done was simple: 'Should he have treated our sister like a prostitute?' (v.31). 'They're not going to mess with us!' was what they were saying. But did that justify the actions they had taken against the whole city? Their desire for justice was wholly understandable, but the way they set about achieving it was reprehensible.

It seems that the horror of what had occurred never left Jacob, because he brought up the subject on his death-bed when Simeon and Levi came to be blessed. Jacob's 'blessing' pronounced upon them was more of a curse, condemning their descendants to be scattered (49:5–7). This was fulfilled when Simeon's descendants were absorbed into the territory of Judah (Josh. 19:1,9), and when Levi's descendants were dispersed throughout the land, living in forty-eight towns and the surrounding pasture-lands (Num. 35:2,7; Josh. 14:4; 21:41).

Are there times when we are so keen to see justice done that we resort to tactics and methods which are inappropriate? Could we be justly criticised for our actions? There may even be occasions when we are tempted to return evil for evil. If so, isn't it better to leave revenge to God, thus avoiding the consequences of such drastic and sinful action? As Paul wrote: 'Do not repay anyone evil for evil ... Do not take revenge ... for it is written: "It is mine to avenge; I will repay," says the Lord' (Rom. 12:17–19). Paul goes on to explain that, rather than revenge, our actions should be the complete opposite, and concludes: 'Do not be overcome by evil, but overcome evil with good' (Rom. 12:20–21).

Goodbye, Joseph! (Genesis 37)

One robe, two dreams

Several years later, Jacob's sons came back Shechem-way with their father's flocks, but then moved on to Dothan. Joseph, who was now seventeen years old, was not allowed to go with them. He was very much his father's favourite, being Rachel's elder son, and Jacob wanted Joseph to stay with him in the camp. Evidently Jacob had learnt nothing from the devastation caused in his own father's household by favouritism (25:28; 27:1–28:5), because here he was, doing the same thing.

The situation had been made far worse by three separate happenings. Joseph had been looking after the flocks with Dan, Naphtali, Gad and Asher, and he 'brought their father a bad report about them' (37:2), which no doubt pleased them no end! Then, Jacob, in his wisdom, visibly flaunted his favouritism for Joseph in front of his other sons, by making 'a richly ornamented robe for him' (v.3). By way of contrast to most of the robes worn in those days, Joseph's was probably like those worn by royalty: long-sleeved rather than short-sleeved; ankle length as opposed to knee length; colourful rather than plain.

Then, to cap it all, Joseph had a dream, which showed all his brothers bowing down before him. Being a tactless teenager, he went and blurted it out to his brothers, who 'hated him all the more because of his dream and what he had said' (v.8). Then Joseph had a second dream. According to Genesis 41:32, a dream that was duplicated meant that it was certain to come to pass. In this second dream, his father and mother were bowing down to him as well as his brothers. He was going to be ruler over them all! Even Jacob thought this was a bit too much, and rebuked Joseph, although he 'kept the matter in mind', while 'His brothers were jealous of him' (v.11).

The plot is hatched

One day, Joseph's brothers were suddenly aware of a figure in the distance approaching them. It wasn't long before they worked out who it was; maybe the robe gave him away. A hasty conference was convened, at which they decided to kill him. "'Here comes that dreamer!" they said to each other. "Come now, let's kill him and throw him into one of those cisterns and say that a ferocious animal devoured him. Then we'll see what becomes of his dreams'" (vv.19–20). Clearly, those dreams still rankled with all of them, and they were determined to put paid to any chance of them coming true, duplicated or not.

But there was one dissenting voice: that of Reuben. As the firstborn son, he would have felt responsible for Joseph. Reuben managed to persuade them not to kill Joseph after all, but suggested that they still threw him into a cistern – presumably so they could take more time deciding what to do with 'that dreamer', as they sarcastically called Joseph.

Publicly, Reuben went along with his brothers' scheme; but privately he intended to rescue Joseph later and take him back to Jacob (vv.21–22). To be fair, Reuben was bold enough to put forward an alternative; but he didn't quite have the courage to stand against the rest of them by suggesting they did nothing at all to Joseph, which he had every right to do as the firstborn.

Do we go along with things in public that we privately disagree with? Do we try to keep our public and private lives separate, when in fact they affect each other? Do we say one thing publicly, and do the opposite in private? If so, won't our lack of integrity be exposed sooner or later, to the detriment of all that we stand for in God? Isn't it better to be consistent in all that we say and do, and take what comes, for the glory of God (Matt. 5:37)?

The deed is done

Joseph had hardly had the chance to greet his brothers when he was seized and thrown into a pit – having been stripped of his symbol of favouritism first (vv.23–24). Later on, while eating their meal, his brothers noticed a caravan of Ishmaelite and Midianite merchants coming in their direction on their way down into Egypt (v.25). The sight of them gave Judah what he must have thought was a brilliant idea. Not only could they get rid of this dreamer for good – but they could make a handsome profit for themselves into the bargain. Perfect! As he said to his brothers when he had gathered them round him: 'What will we gain if we kill our brother and cover up his blood? Come, let's sell him to the Ishmaelites and not lay our hands on him: after all, he is our brother, our own flesh and blood' (vv.26–27). They were all happy enough to follow Judah's lead; and Reuben wasn't around to object – not that they'd have listened to him in preference to Judah anyway.

Presumably it was Judah who went over and negotiated the price for Joseph: twenty shekels of silver. This amount was three years' wages for a shepherd; what a bonus! They yanked Joseph up out of the cistern and handed him over to the merchants, who chained him up ready for his long walk down into Egypt. It would take about thirty days to get there, and then he would be sold as a slave. Joseph's brothers knew that he was unlikely to survive such an experience for very long, particularly as he had led such a pampered life. Although his brothers hadn't actually killed him, they believed they had sent him off to certain death.

But God had other plans in mind for Joseph. Which serves to remind us that, whatever evil people might do, they cannot ultimately thwart God's purposes. No one can put paid to what God has planned. What He has ordained will come to pass; for God is sovereign, is in control, and rules over all (2 Chron. 20:6; Psa. 22:28; 103:19; 1 Cor. 15:25).

The coloured robe

For some unknown reason, Reuben was not with the rest of the brothers when they were selling Joseph to the merchants. When he went to the cistern to get Joseph out, he got the shock of his life. 'The boy isn't there! Where can I turn now?' he wailed to his brothers (vv.29–30). Reuben's plan had completely backfired on him.

Interestingly, Reuben's first response on making the discovery was to think of himself rather than of Joseph. He wondered what would happen to him now, as the firstborn responsible, rather than what would happen to his brother. When difficult situations arise, are we also inclined to think about ourselves first, rather than our thoughts and prayers being with the person most affected?

But Reuben's brothers were too preoccupied to listen to him. They were busy preparing for the scene they were going to play out when they returned to Jacob. Presumably under Judah's direction, they killed a goat, dipped Joseph's robe in the blood, and probably rubbed it in the dirt for good measure (v.31). How they must have enjoyed themselves, as they took that hated symbol and sullied it gleefully.

Back home, they presented the despoiled garment to Jacob. Presumably it was Judah who said, 'We found this. Examine it to see whether it is your son's robe' (v.32). It was all done so coldly and dispassionately – a mark of the depth of their hatred for Joseph, even to the extent of calling him 'your son' rather than 'our brother'. Jacob was completely taken in by their elaborate deception, and drew the conclusions they had hoped for. Jacob, the deceiver, had once again himself been deceived – this time by his sons. Jacob, of course, was beside himself with grief at the thought that his beloved son Joseph had been devoured by a ferocious animal, and refused to be comforted (vv.33–35).

The Tamar incident (Genesis 38)
Levirate marriage

Shortly after this incident, Judah decided to leave the camp of Jacob and strike out on his own. He married a Canaanite woman, and had three sons by her: Er, Onan and Shelah (38:1–5). When Er grew up, Judah found a wife for him; her name was Tamar. But Er died childless, so the principle of Levirate marriage came into play.

This system is explained in Deuteronomy 25:5–10. The reason for it was twofold: to make sure that the dead husband had an heir; to provide care for the widow in her old age. In Tamar's case, she would now marry Onan. Any sons they had would be heirs to his brother Er's estate, and they would care for their mother. It was Judah's responsibility as the father-in-law to make sure that this marriage took place so that the family bloodline would continue, and with it the blessing of the covenant.

In the event, every time Onan had sexual intercourse with Tamar, he made sure she wouldn't bear children as a result. Because he refused to do his duty by his brother and Tamar, he had in fact defied God, and therefore was put to death (vv.8–10). Tamar then went back to live with her father until Shelah was old enough to be married to her (v.11). However, when that time came, Judah failed in his legal obligation to marry Shelah to Tamar, who remained a widow. True, Judah's wife had just died, and he was in mourning for her (v.12), but this hardly excuses his lack of attention to duty. Judah may have been a man of action in his public life, but he seems to have been lacking in his customary decisiveness in his private life at times.

Tamar's trap

The problem for Tamar was that she had no means of legal redress against Judah for not marrying her to Shelah. So she decided to trap him in a way which would bring her justice under the Levirate law and give her a child. The only course of action she could see which would achieve the desired result was to seduce Judah by pretending to be a prostitute.

Having heard that Judah was on his way to Timnah, she dressed herself in such a way that, when Judah saw her, he would think she was a shrine-prostitute (vv.13–15). Having sex with these shrine-prostitutes was encouraged in Canaanite culture, as it was believed to promote fertility in both flocks and crops. They also took a prominent part in festivals and worship of the Canaanite goddesses. These 'public' prostitutes were held in much higher regard than 'private' prostitutes, who could be punished when caught.

Not realising she was his daughter-in-law, Judah propositioned her. Payment of a young goat was agreed for her services, but Tamar also demanded a pledge as a guarantee that the payment would be forthcoming. Judah agreed to Tamar's request that the pledge be his seal, its cord, and the staff in his hand (vv.16–18). The seal was probably a small cylinder which was used to sign clay documents by rolling the seal over the clay. Such seals were hung round the neck with a cord, and were unique to the owner. Having Judah's personal seal in her possession, Tamar could prove beyond all doubt that it was Judah who was the father of the twin sons she would bear as a result of this one-night stand.

Bloodline

After Judah had slept with her, Tamar returned home and dressed herself in her widow's clothes once again. Meanwhile, Judah sent his friend Hirah with the goat for the shrine-prostitute; but she was nowhere to be found. Indeed, the men of the area insisted there had never been a shrine-prostitute there (vv.19–23). Puzzled, Judah returned home. About three months later, Judah was told that Tamar was pregnant. It seemed clear that she must be guilty of prostitution, so Judah's response was: 'Bring her out and have her burned to death!' (v.24).

This seems a bit much, considering Judah himself was guilty of hiring a woman he thought was a prostitute. But in those days, it was more about bloodlines than an issue of morality; and this affected the role of women in society. A wife was expected to bear children for her husband, and to have sexual relations with him alone, so that the family bloodline would be preserved and continued. Therefore, if she committed adultery, she could expect the death penalty, as any children born by extra-marital relations would adulterate the husband's bloodline. But shrine-prostitutes didn't belong to families; so their children were nobody's heirs. This meant, therefore, that men who hired them were not adulterating anybody's bloodline.

So Judah saw no harm in hiring a shrine prostitute for the night; but Tamar deserved death in his eyes because, if she was pregnant due to prostitution, his grandchild would not be part of his family bloodline. For Judah, it wasn't a question of sexual morality; it was a question of keeping his inheritance in the family. So Tamar had to pay the price. Ironically, it was Tamar who had taken action to provide her father-in-law with heirs in the family bloodline, not Judah.

To whom do these belong?

It was now that Tamar played her trump cards. As she was about to be brought out for her public execution, she sent a message to Judah: 'I am pregnant by the man who owns these ... See if you recognise whose seal and cord and staff these are' (v.25). We can only imagine the look on Judah's face as he realised the truth: he himself was the father of Tamar's child; he was about to condemn his own offspring to the flames.

Faced with the awful truth of the matter, Judah admitted publicly that the real fault for what Tamar had done lay with him by saying: 'She is more righteous than I, since I wouldn't give her to my son Shelah' (v.26). Although neither Tamar nor Judah come out of this incident with any credit, Judah seems to suggest that, given the situation, Tamar was more justified in her actions than he was.

In the end, Tamar gave birth to twin boys, Perez and Zerah. Interestingly, the bloodline of Judah continued through the elder of the twins, Perez, who was an ancestor of both king David and Jesus. Even more surprisingly perhaps, Tamar herself gets a mention in the recorded genealogy of Jesus (Matt. 1:3). However, it would be misguided to think that, in view of this, God somehow turns a blind eye to prostitution. Nothing could be further from the truth; such acts are condemned throughout the Bible. Rather, what it does seem to show is how gracious and merciful our God is towards us when we sin against Him (Rom. 5:20–6:2). But, as these verses in Romans make clear, our response to God's grace must be to stop sinning. Have we done this, or are our lives still characterised by wilful sinfulness?

What Judah did may have been culturally acceptable, but he surely knew that such behaviour was not acceptable to God. Could the same be said of us? Are we living in ways that may be the norm in society, but which we know very well are contrary to the teachings of the Bible? When faced with the truth of this, are we prepared to admit that living the world's way is not acceptable to God? Being prepared to admit our mistake, as Judah was, is the first step on the road back to God.

Testing times (Genesis 42–45)
Meeting the governor

The full story of Joseph's dealings with his brothers is beyond the scope of this chapter, but it is interesting to see how the events as they unfolded affected both Reuben and Judah, and the part they played in them.

After his solo excursion, Judah seems to have returned to his father's camp, no doubt wiser and more compassionate than when he left. He was certainly there when famine hit the land, and they were wondering what to do for the best. Jacob was in no doubt as to what they should do. 'Why do you just keep looking at each other?' he said, and told them to get off down to Egypt, where there was apparently plenty of available grain, and buy some (42:1–2).

The governor of the land of Egypt, whom not surprisingly they did not recognise as the brother they had sold to the merchants all those years ago, accused them of being spies, kept Simeon in prison, and demanded they brought their youngest brother with them the next time they came. When the brothers came to the conclusion that all this was happening as punishment for the way they had treated Joseph, Reuben couldn't resist saying, 'I told you so, but you wouldn't listen to me, would you?' (see v.22).

Reuben's offer

When they got back home, they told Jacob that the governor had imprisoned Simeon to make sure that they would return with Benjamin. Jacob was understandably distressed at this news, and didn't want to send Benjamin with them. Benjamin had taken Joseph's place in Jacob's affections as he was Rachel's younger son. Reuben as the firstborn spoke up and said to Jacob, 'You may put both of my sons to death if I do not bring him back to you. Entrust him to my care, and I will bring him back' (v.37).

Jacob flatly refused Reuben's offer (v.38). It seems that, knowing Reuben as he did, he wasn't inclined to trust him. Maybe Jacob had expected Reuben as the firstborn to make sure that no harm would come to Joseph, and felt that Reuben had let him down badly, so he wasn't going to entrust Benjamin to his care. Jacob knew Reuben was full of good intentions in making this offer, but probably doubted whether he would have the courage to stand up to this Egyptian governor, who seemed so intent on making trouble for them all.

Jacob's distrust of Reuben actually went back many years to an incident that occurred before Joseph's disappearance. Jacob found out that Reuben had slept with Bilhah, his own concubine and mother of his two sons Dan and Naphtali (35:22). As his father had never mentioned it, Reuben must have thought he'd got away with his sinful action. But he was wrong. Jacob knew all about it, and brought the subject up on his deathbed (49:4). The result was that Jacob took away Reuben's birthright, and gave his rights as firstborn to Joseph (1 Chron. 5:1–2). Reuben's sin had cost him dear.

All of which serves to remind us that the consequences of our sin can come back to bite us years later. We may think we've got away with it, but we haven't (Num. 32:23). Isn't it better to repent of our sin, and to deal with its ramifications right now (1 John 1:9)?

It seems very likely that Reuben's brothers knew about what he'd done, and had lost total respect for him as leader. They usually paid little attention to what he said, and took decisions without him being there (37:29). Judah became the one they listened to and looked to for leadership; Judah was their spokesperson now. And that is clearly seen in their dealings with Joseph (44:16–34).

Taking responsibility

When the food ran out once again, Jacob knew he had no alternative but to send his sons back to Egypt. This time, Judah offered to guarantee Benjamin's safety. If past events were any guide, this could well mean him finishing up in an Egyptian prison, but Judah was always one to accept and carry out what he perceived as his duty as leader. Jacob seems to have accepted Judah's offer, thus tacitly recognising Judah's leadership position amongst his sons. Judah even had the temerity to suggest to his father that if he'd not been so indecisive, they could have been there and back by now – twice (43:1–10).

Judah was prepared to accept the responsibilities that came with being in a position of leadership. We may not be called to be leaders, but should we not be prepared to commit ourselves to serving God, and take on responsibilities in the work of His kingdom? In my experience, doing this builds character, breeds confidence, causes growth in God, and is both stimulating and motivating. And we know that any work done for God brings great rewards, for God is no one's debtor.

Stirring speech

Once again, Joseph decided to test his brothers, with the result that Benjamin was destined to become the governor's slave. At this point, Judah, as undisputed leader of the group, felt he had to speak out, even though he knew he risked death for being so bold towards the governor (44:16–34). Ironically, the same man whom Joseph had heard, when in the pit, persuading his brothers to sell Jacob's first favourite son into slavery was now pleading the case for Jacob's other favourite son to be saved from the same awful fate, even to the point where he was prepared to go into slavery himself to keep his promise to his father. Judah was showing himself to be a man of his word.

It is clear that, as a result of his experiences, Judah had become a much changed person. Which just goes to show that God can change anyone! So don't let's stop praying for that person whom we've almost given up on; God is able to change them too.

In the event, Joseph was so moved by Judah's stirring speech that he broke down in tears and revealed his true identity to his brothers (45:1–3). He had become convinced by means of the tests he had put them through that his brothers had fundamentally changed for the better during the years that had elapsed since he had last seen them.

Are we courageous enough to speak out under the direction of the Spirit, in spite of the possibility of serious consequences? Who knows what God can do with a voice that is dedicated to Him?

Jacob's blessings (Genesis 49:3-4,8-12)
Reuben

Jacob was reunited with his son Joseph, and spent the rest of his life with him in Egypt. On his deathbed, Jacob summoned his sons so he could bless them. Reuben, the firstborn, would have been expecting a double-portion of the inheritance; but he was in for a shock. His father knew all about his disgraceful behaviour with Bilhah, and Reuben now heard the consequences: he had lost all the blessings of his birthright. How must he have felt as Jacob said to him, 'you will no longer excel, for you went up onto your father's bed, onto my couch and defiled it' (49:4)? He would surely live the rest of his life regretting that moment of madness.

Judah

With Reuben out of the frame, and Simeon and Levi having disqualified themselves due to their actions at Shechem, Jacob officially transferred the leadership aspect of the birthright to Judah, his fourth son (v.8). As we have already seen, the double-portion aspect was bestowed upon Joseph, Rachel's firstborn son.

The lion (v.9) was a symbol of sovereignty, strength and courage. Jesus, who was descended from Judah, was given the title 'the Lion of the tribe of Judah' (Rev. 5:5). The sceptre (v.10) speaks of kingship and power. Judah was the tribe from which most of Israel's kings would come, not to mention the Messiah himself (Micah 5:2). Verses 11 and 12 speak of the prosperity of Judah. In fact, it became the largest tribe, and the southern part of Palestine was known as Judah, and eventually Judea. When the kingdom split in two after the reign of Solomon, the southern part was known as the kingdom of Judah (see Chapters 16–17). The term 'Jew' is also derived from Judah.

Aftermath

When Jacob finally died, Reuben, Judah and their brothers remained in Egypt, provided for by Joseph. They settled in the north-eastern district of the country, in the area called Goshen, where they all eventually died. Their descendants became known as 'the Israelites'. During the next 400 years, they 'were fruitful and multiplied greatly and became exceedingly numerous, so that the land was filled with them' (Exod. 1:7). Then they were made slaves by the Pharaoh, and remained in bondage until God sent Moses to bring them out of Egypt and lead them back to Canaan.

Chapter 5

A Man with a Different Spirit

Caleb

Numbers 13–14
(Other bit part player appearing: Othniel)

Exploring Canaan
The spies are sent out

Having escaped from slavery in Egypt under the leadership of Moses, the Israelites eventually arrived at Kadesh Barnea, an oasis not far from the southern border of Canaan. While they were there, God said to Moses: 'Send some men to explore the land of Canaan, which I am giving to the Israelites' (13:2). This team of spies was to be made up of one representative from each of the twelve tribes. From the tribe of Judah, Moses chose Caleb; and from the tribe of Ephraim he selected Hoshea, to whom he gave the name Joshua (v.16). This same Joshua would become Moses' assistant and the commander of the Israelite army.

Before sending them out to reconnoitre the land, Moses gave the spies a detailed briefing: 'See what the land is like and whether the people who live there are strong or weak, few or many. What kind of land do they live in? Is it good or bad? What kind of towns do they live in? Are they unwalled or fortified? How is the soil? Is it fertile or poor? Are there trees on it or not? Do your best to bring back some of the fruit of the land' (vv.18–20).

Making sure they didn't get caught, the spies carried out a thorough exploration of the land of Canaan in accordance with Moses' briefing. It took them about six weeks to complete their investigation. God had told the Israelites that the land He had promised them would be rich and fertile; a land 'flowing with milk and honey', as it is often described in the Bible. Would the spies' report bear this out?

The spies report back

The people gathered together, presumably with great excitement and anticipation, to hear what the spies had to say. They gave a glowing report about the land, confirming that it did indeed 'flow with milk and honey' (v.27), and proceeded to exhibit some of the wonderful fruit they had brought back. However, the spies reckoned there was a problem; there was a definite 'but' standing in the way (v.28). When the people heard that word 'but' the excited chatter that had undoubtedly broken out among them as they saw evidence of the fruitfulness of the land abated, and a hush descended upon the assembled throng.

The spies went on to explain how there were two aspects to the problem: 'the people who live there are powerful, and the cities are fortified and very large' (v.28). If they entered the land, they would have to deal with the Amalekites, the Hittites, the Jebusites, the Amorites and the Canaanites. And, if that wasn't daunting enough, 'We even saw descendants of Anak there' (v.28), they said. These people were a race of giants, rumoured to be descended from the Nephilim (Gen. 6:4), against whom no one could stand. And as for the cities, they were fortified by walls anything up to twenty-five feet high and twenty feet thick.

The minority report

Not surprisingly, pandemonium broke out among the Israelites. But there was a dissenting voice among the spies. 'Then Caleb silenced the people before Moses and said, "We should go up and take possession of the land, for we can certainly do it"' (v.30). Supported by Joshua, Caleb had the incredible courage and bravery to stand up against the vast majority of the spies and voice his opinion to a now unreceptive crowd.

It's always hard to stand against the majority opinion, isn't it? As Christians living in an increasingly godless and secular society, with laws which undermine what we believe in being proposed almost daily, it's tough to speak out against the prevailing opinion with all its so-called 'political correctness'. Are we prepared to stand up and be counted on these fundamental issues which will affect our nation, or will we remain silent, and let evil triumph?

The other spies turned on Caleb and Joshua, maintaining loudly, 'We can't attack those people; they are stronger than we are' (v.31). By now, the crowd were probably joining in, shouting their opinions. The spies continued to undermine the positive message Caleb had given by persisting with their exaggerated, negative reports about the land of Canaan and its inhabitants. 'The land we explored devours those living in it. All the people ... there are of great size,' they maintained. 'We saw the Nephilim there ... We seemed like grasshoppers in our own eyes, and we looked the same to them' (vv.32–33).

These twelve men were in the same place, at the same time, and saw the same situation; so how could they come to such diametrically opposed conclusions? The reason is that, while the ten spies were walking by sight, Caleb and Joshua were walking by faith. In their account of the exploration, the ten men kept saying 'we saw' (vv.28,32–33), with the result that their report was full of the language of unbelief: 'We can't ... they are stronger' (v.31). Caleb and Joshua, on the other hand, walked by faith, saw by faith, and acted by faith and by contrast, their report is full of the language of faith and belief: 'we can certainly do it ... we will swallow them up ... Do not be afraid' (v.30; 14:9). They were not put off by the obstacles which lay in their path. They were looking at God, not at the problems. Their boldness and confidence was based on what they believed God could do, not on what they believed the Israelites could do.

Had we been one of the spies, how might our reports have sounded? Would they have been full of unbelief, based merely on what we could see, or full of faith, based on our belief in God, no matter what we saw? Paul exhorts us to live by faith, not by sight (2 Cor. 5:7); not to see situations through our natural eyes, but with spiritual vision, and to live accordingly. May God help each one of us to attain this level of maturity in our walk with Him.

Negative talk

The meeting went on all night. There was a lot of shouting, mourning, grumbling and weeping going on. Moses and Aaron came in for a lot of criticism, as usual. The distraught Israelites returned to a familiar theme: 'If only we had died in Egypt! Or in this desert! Why is the LORD bringing us to this land only to let us fall by the sword? Our wives and children will be taken as plunder. Wouldn't it be better for us to go back to Egypt? ... We should choose a leader and go back to Egypt' (14:2–4).

The negative, faithless talk of the ten spies had clearly infiltrated the thinking of the whole camp, and had aroused the emotions of the people to the point where they had got things completely out of perspective. All the things they feared most had come to the surface, and the only solution they could see was to run back to the comparative safety of Egypt as quickly as possible.

What had happened to their faith and trust in the God who had brought them out of bondage, had miraculously enabled them to cross the Red Sea, had wonderfully provided food and water for them in the desert, and whose presence had been with them visibly in the pillars of cloud and fire, protecting them and leading them? Did they really think that God would expect them to accomplish the conquest of Canaan all on their own without any help from Him? Here they were, on the threshold of achieving the goal God had promised them – and they blew it. In the heat and despair of the moment, fear had replaced faith; trust had been ousted by terror; belief had been overcome by unbelief.

Doesn't the same sort of thing happen to us at times? Isn't it true that, while we can trust God to undertake in relatively small matters, we often lose faith when major problems and frightening times loom large in our lives, and distort our perspective? When this happens, it's good to encourage ourselves by remembering all the things that God has already done, and by reminding ourselves that nothing is impossible for Him. God is faithful to His promises (Psa. 145:13), and will enable us to achieve that goal which He has laid on our hearts.

Positive talk

At this point, Caleb and Joshua intervened. They tore their clothes in front of the whole assembly – a symbol of their great distress at what was going on. This seemed to get the crowd's attention. Presumably it was Caleb who then voiced what they were both thinking. Forcefully and courageously, Caleb made the following points: that the land was 'exceedingly good'; that God would lead them into that land and give it to them, provided they did not rebel against Him; that there was no need to fear the people of the land, 'because we will swallow them up'. The inhabitants of the land were defenceless against them, continued Caleb: 'Their protection is gone, but the LORD is with us. Do not be afraid of them' (vv.7–9).

Unfortunately, the assembly did not share their faith-filled vision and confidence in God. The people were so angered that Caleb and Joshua continued to oppose the conclusions drawn by all the other spies, that there was a move to stone the pair of them then and there.

It's easy to criticise the people for being influenced by the majority report, but how often do we come to decisions in a similar way? Are we not frequently swayed by the opinions of experts and friends, rather than making our own judgments? How often is our first question 'What is God saying?' rather than 'What is everybody else saying?'

Consequences

But then the glory of God appeared to the whole assembly (v.10). Moses pleaded with God not to destroy the people, but to forgive their sin. In another act of mercy, God spared the Israelites; but they had to pay a huge price for treating God 'with contempt' (v.11): 'not one of the men who saw my glory and the miraculous signs I performed in Egypt and in the desert ... not one of them will ever see the land I promised on oath to their forefathers. No-one who has treated me with contempt will ever see it' (vv.22–23). This was to apply to all those who were twenty years of age and older (v.29). This unbelieving generation put God's plan back forty years!

God fully vindicated Caleb, and gave him a glowing testimonial (v.24). Caleb would be rewarded for his obedience, his faithfulness, and his wholehearted commitment to God. Joshua also would live to enter the land (v.30); indeed, he would be at the forefront of the invasion. Joshua would eventually lead the children of this generation into the promised land after forty years: 'Your children will be shepherds here for forty years, suffering for your unfaithfulness, until the last of your bodies lies in the desert. For forty years – one year for each of the forty days you explored the land' (vv.33–34). As for the ten spies, their fate was more immediate. Because of their unbelief and their bad report, which had made the people grumble, they 'were struck down and died of a plague before the LORD' (v.37).

Rejected

We know what happened to Joshua, because it is well documented in the annals of Scripture. But what about Caleb? During the years that followed, Caleb had to face up to rejection. He had all the right qualifications for leadership. First of all, he came from the tribe of

Judah, the ruling tribe, unlike Joshua, who was from the minor tribe of Ephraim (13:6,8); so Caleb could well have expected to succeed Moses. Secondly, Caleb was respected by the people. After all, it was Caleb who 'silenced the people before Moses' (13:30), not Joshua. But it was Joshua who was chosen to succeed Moses, not Caleb. Yet it appears that there was never a hint of bitterness in Caleb; he seems always to have supported Joshua fully.

How do we react when someone gets promoted over our head at work, or is given a task in the church which we particularly wanted? Do we allow bitterness to eat us up from within, or do we support that person fully, and look to God for other opportunities?

Commended

God singled out Caleb for special honour among the Israelites: 'But because my servant Caleb has a different spirit and follows me wholeheartedly, I will bring him into the land he went to, and his descendants will inherit it' (14:24).

Caleb was commended by God for his right attitude of mind. There was a 'different spirit' about him in the way he reacted to situations and to people. Caleb seems to have been one of those people who always said or did the right thing. And that was probably because his faith and trust in God was so complete, that he always appeared to see things from God's perspective, to have God's vision, and to know God's mind.

He was also commended for his right attitude of heart. Caleb was totally and utterly committed to God in everything he did; and he still loved and served God, even when things didn't work out as he'd hoped. Caleb would do anything God asked of him with a willing heart, and do it to the best of his ability.

Could God say the same of us: that we have 'a different spirit' and follow Him 'wholeheartedly'? Or are there some areas where our attitudes to situations and people are lacking in godliness, and are no different from those of the world? Does our discipleship and service to God fall short of what it should be? May God help us to show attitudes of mind and heart that are pleasing to Him.

Rewarded

God promised to reward Caleb for his faithfulness and exemplary attitudes: 'Not a man of this evil generation shall see the good land I swore to give your forefathers, except Caleb ... He will see it, and I will give him and his descendants the land he set his feet on, because he followed the LORD wholeheartedly' (Deut. 1:35–36). God always honours and rewards those who stand for Him.

How difficult it must have been for Caleb to endure forty years of frustration in the wilderness with an unbelieving generation before the promise was fulfilled. In my experience, we sometimes have to wait a long time before we see the fulfilment of what God has promised coming to pass in our personal lives, or in the life of our church. Like Caleb, do we maintain an unswerving faith, trust and belief in God throughout that protracted period of waiting? He probably didn't find it easy, any more than we do; but God was with him, because Caleb's heart, mind and eyes were fixed on God (Psa. 141:8).

At last, the time came to cross the River Jordan and enter the promised land. What a thrill that must have been for Caleb after all those years of waiting and anticipation! And as they progressed through the land, Caleb saw his faith in God, expressed to the people all those years ago, being vindicated by one act of God after another: the crossing of the Jordan and the fall of Jericho being just two of them (Josh. 3 & 6). Caleb and Joshua were the only two adults to escape from slavery in Egypt and enter Canaan.

Still serving

Knowing Caleb, he was probably alongside Joshua, whispering words of encouragement, faith and wisdom when they faced setbacks, such as at the town of Ai (see Josh. 8), and in the forefront of the celebrations as they experienced victory. Caleb was eighty-five years old by the time they entered the promised land, but he was still full of life, still full of faith, and still full of fight! When the land had been finally conquered, he came to Joshua to claim the inheritance promised to him by God, saying:

'Now then, just as the LORD promised, he has kept me alive for forty-five years since the time he said this to Moses, while Israel moved about in the desert. So here I am today, eighty-five years old! I am still as strong today as the day Moses sent me out; I'm just as vigorous to go out to battle now as I was then. Now give me this hill country that the LORD promised me that day. You yourself heard then that the Anakites were there and their cities were large and fortified but, the LORD helping me, I will drive them out just as he said.'

Then Joshua blessed Caleb son of Jephunneh and gave him Hebron as his inheritance.

Josh. 14:10–13

What an amazing speech that is. What a tremendous example of faith and trust in God Caleb must have been to the younger generation! Are we who are older such an example to the younger members of our church? Do they look at us and see a faithful servant of God, whose belief and trust in God is unshakable and unwavering, who is still loving God, is still serving God, is still open to God, and is still keen to do exploits for God? In my experience, it is so important to have such examples in our churches. May God help us to be such living testimonies among His people.

Caleb was still serving God with just as much enthusiasm and vigour as ever he had, even though he was now in his eighties. Which just goes to show that we're never too old to serve the Lord! There is no retirement policy in the kingdom of God. There is still a part for us to play in what God is doing. Believing that God would enable and strengthen him, Caleb was determined to lead his clan in driving the Anakites out of the land God had given him, eighty-five years old or not. And drive them out he did: 'From Hebron Caleb drove out the three Anakites ... descendants of Anak. From there he marched against the people living in Debir' (Josh. 15:14–15).

Interestingly, it was Caleb's nephew, Othniel, who captured Debir; his reward was to be married to Caleb's daughter, Acsah

(15:16–17). In response to their requests, Caleb generously gave them a field and springs from which to water it, showing himself to be an approachable and considerate father (15:18–19). Do we display such characteristics towards our own children?

Spiritual heritage

Years later, Othniel became the first of Israel's judges. Because the Israelites had intermarried with the surrounding peoples, and were worshipping their gods, God gave them into the hands of the king of north-west Mesopotamia, Cushan-Rishathaim. After eight years, the Israelites cried out to the Lord, who sent Othniel to deliver them from their oppression, and restore worship of the one true God. It seems that Othniel was one of the few who had remained faithful to God during this time. God's Spirit came upon Othniel in a mighty way to enable him to successfully accomplish his mission; and there was peace in the land for forty years as a result (Judg. 3:1–11).

Clearly, Othniel had learnt a lot from the example of his uncle Caleb. He saw in Caleb something to emulate, and something that was real. How we need such examples in our families as well as in our churches! Are we living testimonies to our relatives that God can use to build up those who know Him, and bring to faith those who don't? And isn't it far more important to leave our families a rich spiritual heritage rather than a rich inheritance of worldly goods? But which of the two do we focus on the more?

A crying need

Today, more than ever, there is a crying need for 'Calebs' in our churches: people with vision, with a different spirit and godly attitudes, with courage and boldness; people who are walking by faith, who are following God wholeheartedly, and who are prepared to fight. Imagine a church full of such people, and what God could accomplish through them …

It's true that we can't all be 'Joshuas'; but we can all be 'Calebs'!

Chapter 6

Trial by Fire

Korah

Numbers 16:1–40
(Other bit part players appearing: Dathan, Abiram, On)

Another uprising

Shortly after the Israelites rebelled over going into Canaan (see Chapter 5), Moses and Aaron faced another uprising. Korah, supported by Dathan, Abiram and On, led his own mini-revolt, challenging both Moses' leadership and Aaron's priesthood. They were backed by 250 council members, well-known and respected leaders in the community.

God had given Moses detailed instructions about the building of the tabernacle, the movable tent where He would be worshipped (Exod. 25–31). Aaron was to be anointed for the sacred office of high priest (Lev. 8). His four sons were to serve in the tabernacle as priests, and would be succeeded in perpetuity by their descendants. The whole tribe of Levi, to which Moses and Aaron belonged, was set apart for service in the tabernacle. As high priest, Aaron was in charge of all the priests and Levites.

Korah himself was a Levite, as were a considerable number of his fellow-rebels. Dathan, Abiram and On were actually from the tribe of Reuben, and presumably had their own grievances against Moses and Aaron. Korah was descended from Levi through his grandfather, Kohath. The Kohathites had especially important duties in the tabernacle, such as caring for the ark of the covenant and the sacred vessels used in the sanctuary (4:1–20); so Korah already had a significant role to play in the service of God. But this was not enough for him. He was obsessively ambitious for the priesthood, and greedy for its power.

Gone too far!

With Korah as their leader and spokesman, they came to confront Moses and Aaron. Korah laid out their complaint: 'You have gone too far! The whole community is holy, every one of them, and the LORD is with them. Why then do you set yourselves above the LORD's assembly?' (v.3). In other words, you're no better than us, we've all been chosen by God, so why should we obey you?

The probable motivation behind Korah's challenge was his passionate belief that he was just as good as Aaron, and could do a much better job of being high priest, given half a chance. It wasn't enough for him to be serving God: Korah wanted to serve God in the highest, most prestigious position. He was more interested in power than in service. Korah would have been fully aware of the powerful role the priesthood played in Egypt, where the priests were rich and politically influential. He clearly hankered after such power and influence for himself.

What Korah couldn't seem to accept was that, although all are equal in God's sight, God Himself chooses those who are to be in positions of leadership – and especially as he wasn't one of the chosen ones. How do we react in a similar situation? Do we challenge God's appointed leaders, especially if we think we're just as good as them and could even do a better job? Or do we get behind them and support them fully with our words, our deeds and our prayers?

Like Korah, are we full of pride, and want to be in a position of power to control others? Or, like Moses, are we humble before God, and only want to be in a position to serve others? There were obviously some 'Korahs' in the church of Paul's day, because he wrote, 'Do nothing out of selfish ambition or vain conceit, but in humility consider others better than yourselves' (Phil. 2:3). As Jesus said, 'For everyone who exalts himself will be humbled, and he who humbles himself will be exalted' (Luke 14:11). Korah was about to discover that there was a price to pay for his insolent arrogance towards God's chosen leaders.

Not content

In reply to Korah's challenge, Moses made it clear that it was not he who had gone too far – it was Korah and his Levite supporters who were guilty of that charge. Moses knew that they had designs on the priesthood (v.10), craving its power, and he wasn't about to ignore their presumption. So Moses set up a trial by fire for the following morning (vv.5–7).

Moses went on to point out to Korah and his fellow Levites that they be content with the privileged ministry that God had called them to, and not consumed with greedy ambition. They were in fact not challenging him, but God Himself; and God would be their judge the following day (vv.8–11).

Korah had many excellent qualities, and God had given him significant responsibilities in His service. The tragedy of Korah is that he was not content with this, and fell prey to his ambition for power. Are we content with the ministry God has called us to? Or, like Korah, are we in danger of wanting to play the part in the work of the kingdom that God has entrusted to someone else, thus allowing ourselves to become discontented in God's service? Are we allowing ambition for a particular position in the church to become an unhealthy obsession? If so, perhaps we need to remind ourselves that God has a particular role and purpose for us to fulfil in His kingdom, and be humble enough to accept the task He has given us to do. Who knows in what ways God will use us in the future if we prove to be faithful in what we are doing for Him right now?

Flaming censers

Even when faced with the prospect of trial by fire, Korah and the Levites showed no inclination to back down. Dathan and Abiram even refused to come and speak to Moses about the situation when he summoned them. They simply sent a message back to Moses accusing him of being a failed and arrogant leader, which not surprisingly made Moses rather angry (vv.12–15)!

The next morning, they all assembled at the tabernacle to see whom God would choose as His priests. In accordance with Moses' instructions they all, including Aaron, brought a censer with them. This was a small bronze vessel in which incense was burnt. Bringing incense was symbolic of coming into God's presence for approval.

So there they all stood, with their censers flaming as the incense burnt, facing Moses and Aaron at the entrance to the Tent of Meeting (vv.17–19). Korah and his followers must have realised the seriousness of their situation, because of what had happened recently to Nadab and Abihu, the two oldest sons of Aaron. They had failed to follow God's instructions when they came to offer incense on one occasion, and were killed by fire from the Lord (Lev. 10:1–2).

The glory of the Lord

Their predicament became all too clear when suddenly 'the glory of the LORD appeared to the entire assembly' (v.19). This was an ominous warning of impending judgment. The Lord did not even acknowledge the presence of Korah and his supporters, speaking only to Moses and Aaron. God told them that He was going to destroy the whole assembly of those who had rebelled. The reaction of Moses and Aaron is quite remarkable, given all that had occurred. They fell down on their faces and pleaded that God would be merciful, and punish only the ringleader (v.22).

God then told Moses to instruct everyone to move away from the tents of Korah, Dathan and Abiram. They were not even to touch anything belonging to them, lest that be taken as a sign that they were siding with these men in their rebellion against God, which would bring them under God's judgment as well (vv.23–26). Moses was at pains to explain to the people that if these rebels died of natural causes, then he was not God's chosen leader; but if God caused the earth to swallow them up, then that was God's judgment upon them for opposing him as their leader, thus vindicating his position (vv.28–30).

Hardly were the words out of Moses' mouth when 'the earth opened its mouth and swallowed them, with their households and all Korah's men and all their possessions. They went down alive into the grave, with everything they owned' (vv.32–33). The rest of the Israelites fled for their lives, lest the earth should swallow them up too (v.34).

Fittingly, the 250 men who had had the temerity to present themselves as priests before the Lord with their censers aflame were consumed by the fire of God (v.35), just as had happened to Nadab and Abihu. Interestingly, the sons of Korah must have had no part in their father's rebellion, because they were not put to death (26:11).

Chilling warning

God commanded that all the censers of the rebels be collected and hammered into bronze sheets to overlay the altar (vv.37–38). The presence of these sheets would serve to remind the Israelites that 'no-one except a descendant of Aaron should come to burn incense before the LORD, or he would become like Korah and his followers' (v.40).

This chilling warning is not the last time Korah's name is to be found in Scripture. He is mentioned again in the epistle of Jude, verse 11, as an example of a man who displayed many of the characteristics and attitudes to be found in those who would seek to mislead the Church, and cause it to rebel against what God has decreed. Like Korah, such people will also face the chilling judgment of God.

Chapter 7

A Life Transformed

Rahab

Joshua 2:1–24; 6:20–25

The house on the wall

At last it was time for the Israelites to come out of the wilderness and possess the land of Canaan. Under the leadership of Joshua, Moses' successor, they camped at a place called Shittim to the east of the River Jordan. Ten miles to the west across the river lay the huge fortress city of Jericho, a major obstacle to their progress. Jericho would have to be taken if they were to march into the land and conquer it.

Joshua needed information about the city and its people in order to plan his attack, so he sent two men to spy out the land and the city. This must have reminded Joshua of the time when Moses had sent him, Caleb and ten others to spy out the land forty years before (see Chapter 5). Whose idea it was for them to hide out in the house of a prostitute isn't clear, but it suited their purpose admirably. Men with no names were coming and going all the time, so the spies would easily be mistaken for clients. It was also a good place to gather information with no questions asked.

Importantly for the spies, the house was built on the wall of the city, giving them a good chance of escape if things went wrong. Such houses were commonplace. The city wall was in fact two walls built twelve to fifteen feet apart. The houses were built on wooden logs laid across the tops of the two walls. Each house had a window looking out over the outside wall.

There is no doubt that God directed them to the house of this particular prostitute, whose name was Rahab (2:1). The spies didn't know it yet, but God knew that Rahab's heart was open to Him, and that she would have a significant role to play in protecting them, updating them, and making their escape possible.

Stacks of flax

When she heard the knock at the door, Rahab must have thought it was just another client, or in this case, two. Rahab may well have realised immediately that they were foreigners by the way they spoke. Maybe it was only later that it dawned on her that they must be Israelites. The Israelite encampment at Shittim was the talk of the city, so it wouldn't have taken Rahab long to work out what these men were probably up to, particularly as they showed no interest in having sex with her, and just wanted a place to stay.

The next thing the spies knew, Rahab was furtively whispering to them to follow her up onto the roof of the house. It seems likely that Rahab had got wind of the fact that one of her clients had sussed out that these two strangers were Israelites, and had informed the king of Jericho. At that time, the main cities of Canaan and their surrounding areas were really small kingdoms, each governed by their own king.

There on the roof, Rahab proceeded to hide the spies under the stacks of flax which were drying up there. Once harvested, flax was piled up on the roof tops to dry in stacks of between three and four feet high. Once dried, the flax was made into yarn, which was then used to make linen cloth. These stacks provided an excellent hiding place for the spies, who must have been asking themselves questions like: 'Why is she doing this? What's she up to? What's in it for her?'

Police raid

Suddenly, there was a fierce pounding on the door. On opening it, Rahab was confronted with a contingent of the city's 'police force' demanding, 'Bring out the men who came to you and entered your house, because they have come to spy out the whole land' (v.3).

Even though they were on the roof, the spies were probably aware of the commotion down below. Their hearts must have been in their mouths, as they wondered whether Rahab would betray them after all. They needn't have worried; Rahab was accomplished in the art of deception. She told the 'police' that it was true the men had been in her house, but that they had left the city at dusk, and she'd no idea where they'd gone or where they came from. She even had the temerity to suggest that they might catch up with the men if they got a move on (vv.4–5).

Rahab had no real alternative but to lie if the spies were to remain undiscovered. She acted for the best in the best way she could, and is commended for her actions: 'was not even Rahab the prostitute considered righteous for what she did when she gave lodging to the spies and sent them off in a different direction?' (James 2:25). However, the Bible makes it clear that such deception is to be the exception rather than the rule (see Chapter 14).

'Melting in fear'

With the police gone, Rahab went back up to the roof to explain herself to the spies. She told them how she and all the people of Jericho were 'melting in fear' (v.9) of the Israelites because of all the exploits their God had wrought, including the crossing of the

Red Sea, and the destruction of the Amorite kings.

Isn't it true that, when God moves mightily, people get to hear about it and know about it? Often the effect of this is to open people up to God. How we need to pray that He will move among us in great power, such that the community around us will know all about it, and be ready to respond to God for themselves! Are we also willing to play our part in telling others about the great things God has done?

What Rahab had heard about God had certainly made a great impact on her life. Indeed, it had brought her from fear of God to faith in Him. Rahab had come to realise that the God of the Israelites was no ordinary God. He was the one true God, the Creator of all, and that resistance to Him was useless. So Rahab pleaded with the spies to save the lives of herself and her family when the city fell to the Israelites, as she was sure it would.

True repentance

Interestingly, although all the people in Jericho were living in fear, it was only Rahab who turned to God in faith for salvation. Cynically it could be said that she only did this because she felt vulnerable to attack, as she was living in a house on the wall: that there was an element of self-preservation in her conversion. But, there is sufficient evidence in Rahab's behaviour to show that her change of heart really was genuine.

For example, consider the risks Rahab took in harbouring and protecting the spies, and helping them to escape. She must have expected the 'police' to return when they failed to track down the spies. Then there is the fact that, after the conquest of Jericho, Rahab lived with the Israelites for the rest of her life (6:25). She changed her lifestyle completely, and lived in accordance with God's laws. She married a man called Salmon, and settled down to a normal family life. She had a son named Boaz (see Chapter 12), who married Ruth. The great-grandson of Boaz and Ruth was King David.

Rahab is the only woman mentioned by name in both the genealogy of Jesus *and* in the portrait gallery of the heroes of faith (Matt. 1:5; Heb. 11:31). The fact that she became an ancestor of the Messiah is an indication of God's seal of approval on the total transformation which took place in the life of this one-time prostitute and sinner. Like Rahab, can people see the truth of our repentance in a changed lifestyle and different attitudes?

Background and regrets

In my experience, God often uses people we wouldn't even consider in order to bring about His purposes. Rahab was a pagan, a Canaanite, a Gentile, and a prostitute! Not a prime candidate for God to use, we might think. But God looks for people with a simple faith and trust in Him, not at their background. It's also easy to fall into the trap of assuming that, because of a person's background, lifestyle or appearance, they won't be interested in hearing about God. Are we ever guilty of not telling someone about God's love for them on those grounds? Are we reaching out to the 'Rahabs' of this world? God wants to transform their lives too.

When she was happily married with a son of her own, Rahab must have had regrets about her past life, but she didn't allow such thoughts to prevent her from serving God. The apostle Paul must also have had similar feelings, considering all the horrors he perpetrated against the Early Church. Presumably he had this in mind when he wrote, 'Forgetting what is behind and straining towards what is ahead, I press on' (Phil. 3:13–14).

Do we allow regrets about our past to prevent us serving God now? Do we consider ourselves unfit for God's service because of what we have done, or because of the background we come from? If so, let's remind ourselves of God's wonderful mercy, grace and forgiveness. Then, like Rahab and Paul, let's leave our past where it belongs – in the past – and 'press on' to serve the God who has loved us and cleansed us from our sins (Rev. 1:5–6).

The scarlet cord

Rahab asked the spies for a 'sure sign' (v.12) that the Israelites would indeed show kindness to her in return for her kindness to them, and that her whole family would be saved. The spies swore an oath to this effect, provided she kept quiet about them, and gathered all her family members into her house when the Israelites entered the land of Canaan. And there was one more thing Rahab was instructed to do: tie a scarlet cord in her window on the outside wall, so her house could be easily identified when they took the city.

This scarlet cord, which guaranteed Rahab's salvation, is symbolic of the sacrifice and shed blood of Jesus, which guarantees our salvation. Rahab's acceptance into the people of God shows that no one, no matter who they are, where they come from, or what they have done, is outside of God's wonderful mercy and grace. Through Christ, anyone can have their life transformed and become a member of the people of God. Can that 'scarlet cord' be seen hanging from our 'windows' as a daily testimony to our faith in Christ, and as a sign of our allegiance to Him?

A test of faith

After she had let the spies down by a rope out of her window on the wall under cover of darkness, Rahab tied the scarlet cord in place. The spies took her advice, and went in the opposite direction to the 'police', hiding out in the many caves in the hills to the west of Jericho. After three days, the 'police' gave up the search, and returned to the city. The spies could now make their way safely back to Shittim, where they reported everything to Joshua, saying, 'The LORD has surely given the whole land into our hands; all the people are melting in fear because of us' (v.24). The fact that the spies used the very phrase Rahab had employed indicates how crucial her assessment of the situation was in instilling confidence into Joshua and the people as they prepared to attack Jericho.

Meanwhile, back in Jericho, Rahab was having to hold her

nerve. The 'police' had returned without finding the spies: would they come back to interrogate her more forcefully? Then the Israelite attack didn't come as soon as she might have expected, and when it did finally materialise, it was nothing like she had anticipated. 'What sort of battle plan is that?' she must have wondered, watching proceedings from the vantage point of her window on the wall; lots of marching and trumpet blowing, but no fighting for six whole days, with apparently nothing to show for it. All around her, the citizens of Jericho were growing in confidence, and deriding the Israelite army. Rather than melting in fear, their fear of the Israelites was itself melting.

What a test of faith as well as nerve this must all have been for Rahab. Did she begin to wonder whether she had done the right thing by turning her back on her own people and going over to the Israelites? Cooped up together in Rahab's house for days on end, did her family begin to question what she had done, and what was, or rather wasn't, going on?

And then, on the seventh day of marching, it all suddenly happened. The walls collapsed, and the Israelite army swarmed into the city, killing every living thing as they went. Presumably Rahab's section of the wall stood firm, because Joshua sent the two spies who'd stayed there to bring her and her family out, as they had promised on oath to do (6:20–25). As Rahab looked back from her place of safety, she could see the city burning. Her old life was over, and her new life was about to begin.

Chapter 8

Sin in the Camp

Achan

Joshua 7

Banned

Before the Israelites swarmed into the flattened city of Jericho, Joshua gave them strict instructions: 'The city and all that is in it are to be devoted to the LORD ... keep away from the devoted things ... Otherwise you will make the camp of Israel liable to destruction and bring trouble on it. All the silver and gold and the articles of bronze and iron are sacred to the LORD and must go into his treasury' (Josh. 6:17–19).

The city of Jericho was the centre of the Canaanite religion, so it came under God's 'ban', His judgment for idolatry. Because God wanted to keep His people holy and free from any idolatrous contamination, He banned them from keeping any loot from the city for themselves. Everything they plundered was to be 'devoted to the LORD': in other words, either destroyed or consecrated to God.

Normally, the Israelite soldiers were allowed to share the plunder of a conquered city, as it provided them with pay, and sustained the army in wartime. But to loot a city under God's ban and keep any of its plunder, no matter how little, was an extremely serious offence, because such an act disobeyed God's explicit command and violated the ban He had imposed.

Getting away with it

One of the Israelite soldiers rampaging through the city of Jericho that day was a man named Achan. In the plunder, he came across some items that took his fancy: 'a beautiful robe from Babylonia, two hundred shekels of silver and a wedge of gold weighing fifty shekels' (7:21). Like everyone else, Achan knew about the ban, but he succumbed to temptation, and secretly took these articles.

Clearly Achan knew very well he was doing wrong by violating God's ban, because he furtively dug a hole inside his tent and hid in it what he had taken. In spite of feeling guilty, Achan obviously thought that what he had done didn't really matter. After all, he may have reasoned, it was only an infinitesimal part of the huge amount of total plunder found in Jericho, and nobody would ever know.

Do we ever commit a sin on similar grounds, believing that our transgression against God's laws is so small and insignificant as to be unimportant? Do we convince ourselves, as Achan seems to have done, that God won't mind, and will overlook what we've done – particularly when we seem to have got away with it? When nothing happened to him or his family, Achan must have thought he had got away with it. But he was in for a shock. His private sin was about to be made public in a spectacular way, with disastrous results all round.

God had warned his people, 'you may be sure that your sin will find you out' (Num. 32:23). All sin matters to God. It does matter what we do with our bodies and with our minds; it does matter how we live, what we say, and how we behave. And somewhere along the line we may be sure that our sinfulness will be exposed; we can't bury it in a hole for ever. Isn't it better to repent and put things right, thus avoiding what could be serious consequences, not only for ourselves, but for other people too?

Crushing defeat

After the conquest of the huge fortress of Jericho, Joshua must have thought that taking the much smaller city of Ai was going to be a breeze. So much so, that he didn't speak to God about it, and was therefore totally unaware that 'the LORD's anger burned against Israel' (v.1). In my experience, consulting God before we do anything, even when we are on a spiritual 'high', is essential to avoid the possibility of making costly mistakes. How often are we prone to rely on our own resources and abilities, especially when the task appears to be easy and straightforward, only to find ourselves in dire straits… just as Joshua was about to?

It was strategically important for the Israelites to capture Ai, because it would give them a base in the central highlands of the country. Otherwise, they would remain vulnerable to attack in the Jordan valley, where the river effectively cut off any possibility of retreat. The spies Joshua sent to reconnoitre Ai reported that a small force of between 2,000–3,000 men would be quite sufficient to complete the task (vv.2–3). In the event, 'they were routed by the men of Ai, who killed about thirty-six of them' (vv.4–5). Clearly, the soldiers of Ai were not quaking in their boots because of what had happened at Jericho. This crushing defeat had a profound psychological effect on the Israelites: 'the hearts of the people melted and became like water' (v.5). It was an unmitigated disaster.

Drastic measures

Joshua now did what he should have done before the attack on Ai – he came before the Lord in prayer, accompanied by the elders. They came to the tabernacle in mourning, their clothes torn and dust sprinkled on their heads. They fell down on their faces in humility before the Lord, and Joshua poured out his heart to God. His main concern was the encouragement this disaster at Ai would give to their enemies to oppose their advance, and seek to wipe them out.

Although he never said it out loud, uppermost in Joshua's mind as he talked to God must have been the question 'Why?' God answered his unspoken enquiry: 'Israel has sinned; they have violated my covenant, which I commanded them to keep. They have taken some of the devoted things; they have stolen, they have lied, they have put them with their own possessions ... That which is devoted is among you, O Israel. You cannot stand against your enemies until you remove it' (vv.11,13). Failure to do this would mean that God would no longer be with them (v.12).

Drastic measures were required. Because they had sinned, the Israelites had to be purified, and go through the prescribed rites to bring this about. Then, there was to be a public exposure and public judgment of the sin that had contaminated them all.

Corporate responsibility

The sin of one man, Achan, had brought judgment on the whole nation. Why was this? Probably because God needed the Israelites to grasp the concept of corporate responsibility at this time: that they were not a collection of individuals, but one body, charged with the task of conquering Canaan under God's direction and according to His instructions. Just one person disobeying God's commands could jeopardise the whole campaign. God required them to be His holy people, and to take on the responsibility of being so committed to one another and to the cause, that they no longer regarded themselves as individuals, but as a body, whose every move affected everyone else.

Isn't it the case that each one of us has a responsibility to the Body of Christ, the church where we worship? God is looking for a people who are characterised by holiness and obedience (John 14:23; 1 Pet. 1:15). Could it be that our personal acts of sinfulness and disobedience are preventing God from blessing in full measure the body we are a part of?

Judgment day

Did Achan connect the disaster at Ai and the death of thirty-six men with his act of disobedience? When he was undergoing the purification rites that night with all the rest of the people, did the thought ever cross his mind that all this was his fault? Did he ever realise that his sin had affected the whole camp, that he alone was responsible for all this trauma? If so, he kept very quiet about it.

And what about early the next morning, when Joshua gathered all the people together in their tribes? Surely Achan must have realised by now that something drastic was happening! But he still kept quiet, even when his tribe, Judah, then his clan, the Zerahites, and then the family of Zimri, to which he belonged, were singled out by the casting of lots. Each man in the family of Zimri had to step forward in front of Joshua, and the lot fell on Achan. The time for keeping quiet was over (vv.16–18).

Achan blurted it all out to Joshua, even telling him where he had buried the goods. Joshua sent men to retrieve these 'devoted things', and took them, along with Achan, his family and all his possessions, to a place which would become known as the valley of Achor. Joshua said to Achan, 'Why have you brought this trouble on us? The LORD will bring trouble on you today' (v.25). Then they were all stoned to death, because Achan had violated God's command, and their bodies and belongings were burnt to purge the land of the evil (vv.19–26). With Israel now cleansed from sin and restored to God, Joshua attacked Ai again, and this time the Israelites were victorious (8:1–29).

Whether they were involved in his sin or not, the whole of Achan's family paid the price for his disobedience. In those days, families were regarded as one unit, with the head of the family being its chief. If he was guilty of something, so were all his family. Achan's sin and any vestige of it had to be cut out of the body of

God's people, which therefore necessitated the death of his family as well as himself. This only serves to remind us again of the drastic consequences sin can have, often upon the innocent.

The valley of Achor

The name 'Achan' is similar to the Hebrew verb 'akar', which means 'to distress' – rather appropriate, considering all the turmoil his actions had caused. In a play on words, Joshua gave this valley of death the name 'Achor', which means 'disaster' or 'trouble'. The prophets Hosea and Isaiah both referred to it in later years.

Hosea told the people of the northern kingdom that if they repented and were restored to God, then there would be hope in the face of the disaster they were facing. God would 'make the Valley of Achor a door of hope' (Hosea 2:15). But they didn't listen, and were conquered by the Assyrians.

Over a century later, the people of the southern kingdom were carried off into exile by the Babylonians. There in exile, Isaiah had a vision of how God was going to transform this disaster: 'Sharon will become a pasture for flocks, and the Valley of Achor a resting place for herds, for my people who seek me' (Isa. 65:10). God promised that what was a God-forsaken disaster would be transformed into a place of divine habitation.

Isn't it encouraging to know that the valley of trouble and disaster is the place where we can experience the presence of God in a mighty way, have our hope restored, and see the situation transformed? And, as David reminds us, even in the valley of death I have no need to fear, 'for you are with me' (Psa. 23:4).

Chapter 9

God's Left-hand Man

Ehud

Judges 3:12–30
(Other bit part player appearing: Eglon)

Invasion and occupation

After the time of Israel's first judge, Othniel (see Chapter 5), the Israelites once again 'did evil in the eyes of the LORD' (3:12). The result of this was that they came under the power of Eglon, king of Moab. Eglon persuaded the Ammonites and Amalekites to join him, and together they invaded the area of Israel around Jericho (v.13). Having captured the city, Eglon took up residence in Jericho and made it his headquarters.

The Moabites and Ammonites were descendants of Lot (see Chapter 1), and the Amalekites had Esau as their ancestor (Gen. 36:12,16). They were nomadic tribes who lived to the east and south-east of Canaan, and had a fearsome reputation as raiders.

Unlikely deliverer

The Israelites were subject to Eglon for eighteen years (v.14). Whether the people 'cried out to the LORD' during or after that length of time isn't clear; but God heard their cry and 'gave them a deliverer' (v.15). That deliverer, who would become the second judge of Israel, was a man called Ehud.

As far as the Israelites were concerned, Ehud would have been a rather unlikely choice for such a role, simply because he was left-handed! In those days, being left-handed was regarded as a weakness and a handicap. Interestingly, many men from Ehud's tribe, the tribe of Benjamin, were left-handed (Judg. 20:15–16). But God was about to use a man with this perceived weakness to carry out His purposes. Indeed, Ehud's very left-handedness would give him the advantage over his enemy.

In my experience, God sometimes uses people we consider unlikely to have an impact in a particular area of service in His kingdom to confound us by doing exactly that! And when that happens, doesn't it serve to remind us that everything that is accomplished for God is achieved through His grace and strength, and not through our own human endeavour?

Tribute and trickery

This particular year, Ehud was sent as the representative of the people to pay the annual tribute to King Eglon. The tribute probably took the form of agricultural produce, and therefore several men were needed to carry it. Ehud saw this occasion as an opportunity to free his people from the rule of this king of Moab, and decided exactly how he would go about it.

Ehud fashioned a purpose-made weapon just the right length to strap to his thigh, where it would be concealed under his clothing. The weapon is described as 'a double-edged sword about a foot and a half long' (v.16), so we would think of it more as a dagger. When the tribute had been presented to Eglon, Ehud sent the men who had come with him away first, before making out to set off for home himself. However, when he reached the stone statues marking the boundary of the king's territory near Gilgal, Ehud turned round and went back to Eglon's palace to put the next stage of his plan into operation.

Ehud now tricked Eglon into being alone with him. He told Eglon: 'I have a secret message for you, O king' (v.19). On hearing this, Eglon dismissed all his attendants, as Ehud had anticipated he would. His plan was working beautifully. The two of them were now alone together in the upper room of the palace. Ehud then said, 'I have a message from God for you' (v.20). As Eglon got to his feet, Ehud drew out the dagger from his right thigh with his left hand. This move would have taken Eglon completely by surprise, as weapons were usually drawn from the left-hand side of the body by the right hand. Had Eglon's attendants previously checked Ehud's left-hand side for a weapon, not realising that he was left-handed?

With Eglon caught completely off-guard, it was an easy task for Ehud to plunge the dagger into the king's stomach with his left hand. Eglon was 'a very fat man' (v.17), so fat that 'Even the handle sank in after the blade, which came out of his back ... and the fat closed in over it' (v.22). What a grotesque picture that conjures up!

New hero

Now Ehud had to act quickly. He slipped out of the upper room, locked the doors behind him and, taking the key with him, made good his escape. When Eglon's servants returned and found the doors locked, they assumed that Eglon had gone to the toilet, so they waited. This gave Ehud even more time to get away and put the next part of his plan into action. Eventually the servants realised something was up; so they got a key and went in, to find their king dead on the floor.

Meanwhile, Ehud had blown a trumpet to summon the Israelites to assemble for a fight. "'Follow me," he ordered, "for the LORD has given Moab, your enemy, into your hands"' (v.28). Ehud now showed himself to be a very shrewd military tactician. By 'taking possession of the fords of the Jordan' (v.28), the Israelites killed two birds with one stone – they stopped the Moabites fleeing the Jericho area from escaping across the river to safety in Moab and, at the same time, prevented reinforcements arriving from Moab. The result was a great victory for Israel with 10,000 Moabites killed, followed by eighty years of peace under the leadership of their new unlikely hero: the left-handed Ehud.

Is it possible that God wants to use what we, and maybe others too, have seen up to now as a weakness in our make-up to bring about His purposes? As in the case of Ehud, maybe that perceived weakness is just what God needs to use right now for the furtherance of His kingdom right where we are.

Chapter 10

The Bee and the Thunderbolt

Deborah

Judges 4
(Other bit part players appearing: Barak, Sisera, Heber, Jael)

The Canaanites are back!

After the death of Ehud (see Chapter 9), it was back to the same old story: 'the Israelites once again did evil in the eyes of the LORD' (4:1). The result was that they were defeated by Sisera, the commander of the army of Jabin, a king of Canaan. This was the only time in the period of the judges when Israel was attacked by an army from within its own borders.

The Israelites had disobeyed God's instructions in the past to drive the Canaanites out of the land, and this failure had now come back to haunt them. Over the years, the beleaguered Canaanites had got their act together, and were determined to take back control of what they regarded as being their land. A mark of their power was the 900 iron chariots at Sisera's command, against which the Israelite army, disunited as it was, had little chance. The huge number of chariots also suggests that there was a confederation of Canaanite cities working together under the military leadership of Sisera, who was not actually a Canaanite himself.

It seems unbelievable that the Israelites tolerated this cruel oppression for twenty years before crying out to God (v.3). And yet, are there not times in our own lives when God is our last resort rather than our first port of call? Like the Israelites, are we not prone to try and sort out matters in our own strength, and finish up getting ourselves in a mess? As the hymn-writer, Joseph Scriven, said, 'O what peace we often forfeit, O what needless pain we bear, all because we do not carry everything to God in prayer'.

Exceptional

Married to Lappidoth, Deborah, whose name means 'bee', was the acknowledged leader of Israel at the time. She must have been an exceptional woman, showing outstanding leadership skills and judicial wisdom, to find herself in such a position in what was very much a man's world. Indeed, Deborah is the only one among all the judges also to be described as a prophet(ess). This is indicative of her close, personal relationship with God.

The example of Deborah reminds us that God can choose anyone he pleases for a leadership position, male or female, young or old, charismatic or reserved. When it comes to leaders, are we guilty at times of challenging or delaying God's plans due to our own prejudices and preferences?

Maybe it was at Deborah's instigation that the Israelites turned to prayer. Certainly it was shortly after they cried out to the Lord that God spoke to her. In typical style, Deborah took decisive action. She summoned Barak, whose name means 'thunderbolt'. He was the leader of the Israelite army, but was living in a town subject to Canaanite rule. Deborah told Barak that God's instructions were for him to take 10,000 men to Mount Tabor. Meanwhile, God would lure Sisera and his forces into the valley of Jezreel along the Kishon river, and give Sisera into Barak's hands.

Never mind the chariots ...

Barak was distinctly underwhelmed by this proposition. Perhaps he had got used to living under Canaanite oppression, and was prepared to live with it rather than risk making it worse. Maybe he was just a weak character, and not a 'thunderbolt' at all; more of a damp squib! Or did it just boil down to the superior size of Sisera's army with the 900 iron chariots at his disposal – quite enough to decimate most armies, never mind the Israelite one. Whatever the case, Barak wasn't prepared to step out in faith on his own. He insisted that Deborah went with him. Perhaps Barak thought that her presence as a prophetess of God would guarantee God's presence too.

Deborah, being the strong leader that she was, and full of faith in God to accomplish what He had promised, no matter what the odds, immediately agreed to go with Barak. This woman was a 'bee' with a real sting! Deborah went on to say that, because of his lack of faith, God had decreed that Barak would not get the honour for the victory. Rather, Deborah prophesied, the honour would go to the woman into whose hand the Lord would deliver Sisera.

Deborah didn't look at the circumstances: she looked at God. In my experience, that can be difficult to do. Sometimes the circumstances assume such large proportions that any sight of God seems to get blocked out. How important it is to follow Deborah's example and 'fix our eyes on Jesus' (Heb. 12:2) – to look beyond the situation to our almighty God, and put our trust in Him. Then problems take on a new and different perspective. Years later, King David would write these words, with which I'm sure Deborah would have wholeheartedly agreed, given the 900-chariot situation she was facing: 'Some trust in chariots and some in horses, but we trust in the name of the LORD our God' (Psa. 20:7).

Into battle

The Israelite army duly made its way to Mount Tabor, and took up position on the mountain slopes, safe from any chariot attack. Meanwhile, Sisera had received information on the whereabouts of the Israelite army from a man named Heber, a Kenite. The Kenites were descended from relatives of Moses, and had always allied themselves with Israel. However, seeing the way the wind was blowing, Heber and his clan had defected to the Canaanite side (vv.11,17).

Sisera probably couldn't believe his luck when he heard Heber's news. The valley of Jezreel, which lay at the foot of Mount Tabor where the Israelite army was stationed, would become the battlefield, and it was perfect ground for his chariots, allowing plenty of room for manoeuvre. Accordingly, he lined them all up along the Kishon river in the valley (vv.12–13). But, in his arrogance, Sisera had reckoned without God. He had fallen into the trap God had prepared for him.

Meanwhile, back on the mountainside, Deborah commanded Barak, 'Go! This is the day the LORD has given Sisera into your hands. Has not the LORD gone ahead of you?' (v.14). Interestingly, storms were frequent in the valley of Jezreel, and often caused the river to flood, making it impassable. In April 1799, the Kishon river flooded, helping Napoleon defeat a Turkish army in that very valley.

Although a storm is not mentioned, something must have happened because the chariots were rendered ineffective. Sisera even abandoned his, and fled from the battlefield on foot, while Barak and his men pursued and massacred the Canaanite forces (vv.15–16). The 'thunderbolt' finally lived up to his name! Interestingly, the Hebrew word translated 'routed' (v.15) was the one used to describe the panic that overcame the Egyptians at the Red Sea when their chariots were rendered useless (Exod. 14:24).

Enter the goat

Meanwhile, Sisera found himself at the camp of Heber the Kenite. This must have come as a great relief to him, because here he could surely hide in safety from any pursuing Israelites. Jael, the wife of Heber, recognised Sisera as soon as he arrived on the scene, and went out to meet him. Presumably he recognised Jael as the wife of his new-found ally Heber, and willingly put himself in her hands. Jael took Sisera into her tent, which must have made him feel even more secure. According to the custom of the day, no man other than the woman's husband or father was allowed to enter her tent, so Sisera would have been confident that no one would think of looking for him in there.

However, unbeknown to Sisera, or her husband, Jael had remained secretly loyal to the Israelites. When Sisera asked for a drink of water, Jael, whose name means 'mountain goat', gave him some goats' milk instead. The exhausted Sisera soon fell fast asleep, and Jael seized her chance with great courage and resolve. In those days, it was the woman's job to pitch the tent, so Jael was quite familiar with driving tent pegs into the ground. Picking up a tent peg and a hammer, Jael crept to where Sisera lay sleeping. Keeping her nerve, she placed the peg on his temple, and 'drove the peg through his temple into the ground, and he died' (v.21).

Shortly afterwards, Barak arrived in the camp searching for Sisera. Jael went out to meet him, and took him to see the body of the man he had feared. There lay the great commander with a tent peg through his head. Sisera must have hoped to meet a glorious death in battle at the hand of the enemy; but instead he had suffered an ignominious death in a tent at the hand of a woman. With the death of Sisera, the Canaanite alliance collapsed, and the Israelites gradually regained control of the country.

As was traditional in the culture of Israel, great victories were celebrated in song, and this occasion was no exception. The triumphal song recorded in Judges 5 could well have been written by Deborah herself. The singing was led by Deborah and a transformed Barak. As Deborah had prophesied, special honour in the song was given to the woman into whose hand the Lord had delivered Sisera – Jael, the wife of Heber the Kenite (5:24–27).

A servant of God

In spite of her exalted position, Deborah had a servant heart. She did not yearn for power, or exploit it for her own ends. She didn't allow the fact that she was a woman and a wife to inhibit her from serving God to the full. She was always open to God, and gave Him all the glory and praise. She was courageous in the face of the enemy, and was sensitive to what God was saying. She showed great wisdom in both her judgments and in her role as leader.

What a challenge she presents to all of us! No matter who we are, or what position we hold, may God help us to be like Deborah: a wise, courageous, God-honouring, sensitive, wholehearted servant of God.

Chapter 11

A Man of His Word

Jephthah

Judges 10:6–12:7
(Other bit part player appearing: Jephthah's daughter)

Oppression

The next leader and judge after Deborah was Gideon, who subdued the Midianites and brought forty years of peace to Israel (Judg. 6–8). After his death, there was a period of violence and slaughter as Abimelech, Gideon's illegitimate son, established himself as ruler for three years. Abimelech was followed first by Tola, who led Israel for twenty-three years, then by Jair, who was their leader for twenty-two years (Judg. 10:1–5).

Jair's death was followed by a period of uncertainty, and 'Again the Israelites did evil in the eyes of the LORD' (v.6a). They worshipped the gods of their neighbours, and God in His anger allowed the Philistines and the Ammonites to crush the Israelites. After eighteen years of this oppression, the Israelites repented before the Lord, got rid of all the foreign gods, served God and submitted themselves to His will, beseeching Him to deliver them from their oppressors. Moved by His people's misery, God in His mercy came to their rescue.

The outcast returns

Faced by the prospect of a new offensive by the Ammonites (see Chapter 1), the elders of Gilead, the area now under threat, decided to send for Jephthah (11:4–5). He was the firstborn son of a man named Gilead, but his mother was a Canaanite prostitute. Gilead's other sons by his wife had driven their illegitimate brother out of the area, maintaining that Jephthah had no part in their father's inheritance.

Jephthah was cast out by his family, through no fault of his own. Are we guilty of driving people away from our churches, simply because they don't fit in with the way we do things, or with what we perceive as the norm? We may not even realise we're doing it. Perhaps we need to ask ourselves how we can make sure this isn't happening, and how we can make people from all backgrounds and situations feel welcome in our midst and included in our activities.

Jephthah had taken refuge in the land of Tob, which lay to the north of Gilead. Both lands lay to the east of the River Jordan. There he was joined by 'a group of adventurers' (v.3), who made him their leader. Jephthah soon gained a reputation as a 'mighty warrior' (v.1), presumably by leading this gang of disreputables in raids on the enemies of Israel. The elders of Gilead saw this native outcast as the ideal man to return and lead them in battle against the Ammonites.

But Jephthah wasn't all that keen on the idea, and probably thought it was a bit of a cheek, considering how he had been treated. They had had no compunction about throwing him out; but now they were in trouble, they wanted him back! Jephthah was quite happy where he was, and was suspicious of the overtures being made to him by the elders. They had driven him out of

Gilead before; would they not do so again, once the battle was won? Not surprisingly, Jephthah needed a lot of convincing that the elders' offer to make him commander of their forces and ruler over the land was genuine and lasting. The elders were so desperate for Jephthah to return that they swore an oath confirming their proposals, and he was publicly proclaimed tribal leader in a religious ceremony conducted in front of the army gathered in Mizpah (vv.7–11).

Diplomacy

Thus firmly established in his position, Jephthah attempted a diplomatic dialogue with the Ammonites. He sent messengers to their king asking why he was attacking Israel again. The king reckoned that when Israel had originally arrived on the scene from Egypt, they had taken possession of land rightfully belonging to Ammon.

Jephthah replied, repudiating this claim. He pointed out that the land in question had in fact been taken from the Amorites, not the Ammonites (vv.16–22). Jephthah maintained that it was Israel's God who had given that land to Israel, and that nobody had questioned Israel's possession of it for 300 years! Just as Ammon was entitled to the land given it by their god, so the land given to Israel by their God belonged to them (vv.23–26). This meant that Ammon had no justification whatever for waging this war, and if the king persisted, he would come under the judgment of the one true Judge (v.27). In so saying, Jephthah was acknowledging that he was placing his faith and trust in God to deliver His people from the vastly superior Ammonite forces. Jephthah's faith in God is recognised, as he is mentioned by name in the portrait gallery of faith (Heb. 11:32).

Jephthah was prepared to give peace a chance in his relationships with others. Are we? Jesus said, 'Blessed are the peacemakers', and commanded us to 'be at peace with each other' (Matt. 5:9; Mark 9:50). This theme continues through the New Testament. If we are not living in peace with everyone, we are exhorted to take the initiative, do something about it, and be reconciled to the person or people concerned. In my experience, this is often easier said than done, but is something Jesus expects of us as His disciples.

A rash vow

It soon became clear that Jephthah's attempt to settle matters peacefully had been a failure (v.28), so he began to prepare for the inevitable war. It was at this point that 'the Spirit of the LORD came upon Jephthah' (v.29), empowering him supernaturally for the task and the responsibilities to which God had called him. The rejected man had become God's chosen deliverer. Jephthah then passed through the lands of Gilead and Manasseh gathering reinforcements to fight the Ammonites.

On the eve of the battle, Jephthah made a vow to God. This was a common practice in those days before battle was joined. However, what was unusual about this vow was the fact that Jephthah explicitly promised that, should the Ammonites be defeated, a sacrifice would be made as a burnt offering to God: '… whatever comes out of the door of my house to meet me …'(vv.30–31). The wording of the vow is somewhat ambiguous: 'whatever' (v.31) can equally well be rendered 'whoever'.

There has been much speculation about the intention of this vow, but it seems more likely that Jephthah had a human rather than an animal sacrifice in mind, even though God had expressly forbidden the former (Lev. 18:21). If that were indeed the case, then Jephthah had allowed himself to be influenced by the practices of the nations around him, almost all of whom regularly offered human sacrifices. Perhaps he thought that the God in whom he trusted for victory deserved as high an accolade as his enemy's god would receive were they to be victorious. Whatever Jephthah's reason or intention may have been, it would turn out to be a very rash vow indeed.

The battle against the Ammonites itself only gets a very brief mention: 'the LORD gave them into his hands. He devastated twenty towns ... Thus Israel subdued Ammon' (vv.32–33). It is the consequences of Jephthah's rash vow that are given the full treatment, and serve as a warning that God is not to be bargained with in such a way.

Do we ever find ourselves bargaining with God in our prayers, or making rash promises to Him in the heat of the moment? Do we ever hear ourselves saying things like, 'Lord, if you get me out of this situation, I will ... '? If we make such vows, let's be under no illusions that God will expect us to keep them. But isn't it encouraging to know that there's no need to bargain with God? All He wants us to do is to simply put our faith, trust and confidence in Him.

Utter horror

To Jephthah's utter horror, the 'whatever' proved to be a 'whoever': his only daughter. Returning to his home town of Mizpah in triumph, 'who should come out to meet him but his daughter, dancing to the sound of tambourines! She was an only child. Except for her he had neither son nor daughter' (v.34). It was customary for women to greet victorious armies returning from battle in this manner, and there she was, leading the way.

We can hardly begin to imagine how Jephthah must have felt when he saw her. He may well have been expecting one of his slaves or servants to emerge first, but instead it was his only daughter. Would he keep his vow now, or would he renege on it? Whatever we may think of Jephthah, he was a man of his word, even though it was going to cost him total grief and despair. Tearing his clothes as an expression of his grief, he cried out, 'Oh! My daughter! You have made me miserable and wretched, because I have made a vow to the LORD that I cannot break' (v.35). What tears and sobs must have accompanied these desperate words.

Are we known as people who keep our word, no matter what the cost to ourselves turns out to be? Can others rely on us to be where we've promised to be, to do what we've promised to do, to say what we've promised to say? If not, then surely that means our lives are lacking integrity. And that not only reflects badly on us, but more importantly on the gospel we proclaim, and on the Lord whom we serve.

Innocent victim

The real tragedy of this affair is that it needn't have happened at all. Jephthah had no need to make any vow, never mind such a one as this, in order to secure God's favour. Jephthah's expression of faith and confidence in God to decide the outcome of the battle would have been sufficient. Interestingly, God did not intervene to let Jephthah off the hook. He had made the vow of his own free will, and was required to see it through.

The reaction of Jephthah's daughter to her father's words was nothing short of amazing, and probably not what Jephthah was expecting at all. She understood the situation completely, and was totally willing to comply with her father's rash vow: 'you have given your word to the LORD. Do to me just as you promised' (v.36). There were no recriminations, no emotional outbursts, no cutting words of reproach; just a calm acceptance of her fate.

This young woman, with her whole life before her, was the innocent victim in this whole tragedy, and we don't even know her name. Her plight, however, was to be remembered by the young women of Israel in the future (vv.37–40). How many other people, whose names we don't know either, are victims of persecution today all across this world, simply because they dare to confess Jesus as Lord? Their undying faith in God, their total love for Him, and their calm acceptance of its consequences, puts many of us to shame. Do we remember them in prayer, and consider the sacrifice they are being called upon to make?

Confrontation and pronunciation

Instead of producing joy unconfined across the land of Israel, Jephthah's victory only resulted in pettiness, squabbling, old jealousies resurfacing, and ultimately confrontation. The tribe of Ephraim, who at that time seem to have considered themselves to be the natural leaders of Israel, were not willing to accept a Gileadite like Jephthah as judge. In fact, they had also caused trouble for Gideon in the past (8:1–3). The Ephraimites reckoned that Jephthah hadn't asked them to fight in the battle, so they threatened to burn his house down, and used various insulting words about his tribe (12:1,4). Jephthah firmly denied the charge, implying that the Ephraimites didn't come because they were too scared (v.3).

Once again, Jephthah tried to avoid bloodshed by talking to the Ephraimites, but to no avail. Jephthah soon realised that there was only going to be one effective way to quash this rebellion, so he took the required decisive action (v.4). He and his men captured the fords of the River Jordan which separated Ephraim from Gilead. As the surviving Ephraimites tried to escape back across the fords to their land in the west, the Gileadites would stop them. If they denied being Ephraimites, they were required to say the word 'Shibboleth'. The fact that they couldn't properly pronounce the 'sh' sound gave them away, and they were promptly put to death (vv.5–6).

The upshot of this slaughter of the Ephraimites was that the tribes to the west of the Jordan quickly submitted to the leadership of Jephthah, who went on to lead and judge the whole of Israel for six years (v.7). Jephthah showed himself to be as hard with his fellow Israelites, the tribe of Ephraim, as he was with his enemies, the Ammonites – not to mention with himself. Jephthah was a man of his word, and proved to be the strong leader the nation needed during the short time he was in charge.

Chapter 12

Doing What's Right

Boaz

Ruth 2–4
(Other bit part players appearing: Elimelech, Mahlon, Kilion, Orpah)

First encounter (Ruth 2)
Bethlehem

The book of Ruth is made up of four chapters, each of which is like an act in a play or drama. The story told in the book took place during the time of the judges (1:1), dark and desperate days in the history of the Israelites, when 'everyone did as he saw fit' (Judg. 21:25). The events described in Ruth shine like a beacon in this darkness, showing selflessness, integrity and faith in God, in an age of self-centredness, immorality and apostasy. God was still at work, even in times such as these.

Boaz, a rich, successful farmer and landowner from Bethlehem, first appears in Act Two. The name 'Boaz' probably means 'in him is strength'. He is described as 'a man of standing' (2:1), implying that he was well thought of and looked up to in the town, as well

113

as being a man of property. The town of Bethlehem lay about six miles to the south-west of Jerusalem. It was surrounded by fertile land, which produced abundant harvests, and plentiful olive groves. The climate allowed for two barley and wheat harvests each year, in the spring and in the autumn.

The corn in the corners

It was the time of the spring barley harvest, and Boaz arrived from Bethlehem to see how his workers were getting on in the field. His greeting to them, 'The LORD be with you!', and their reply, 'The LORD bless you!' (v.4), sound more like words heard in a place of worship than in a place of work! It was an indication that both master and workers recognised their reliance on God for His provision of the harvest. This friendly interchange also suggests that Boaz had an excellent relationship with his employees, and that they respected him greatly.

Reapers were employed at harvest time. Usually, the men cut down the stalks of grain, and the servant girls tied them into bundles, which were then taken to the threshing floor. However, in Israelite fields, the corn in the corners would be left uncut, and any grain dropped in the process of tying the bundles would be left on the ground. The poor and needy of the community could then come along and gather the grain that had been left behind, a process called 'gleaning', and feed themselves. The requirements concerning this welfare provision for the destitute were set out in the Law of Moses, and promised blessing to farmers who showed their generosity in this way (Lev. 19:9; 23:22; Deut. 24:19). Boaz, a man who was known for doing what was right, made sure that the law was observed on his land.

Looking round his field, Boaz suddenly caught sight of a young woman, whom he didn't recognise, gleaning busily. The sacrifice that Ruth had made in leaving her homeland of Moab to accompany her mother-in-law Naomi back to Bethlehem and look after her had obviously impacted the local community, because Boaz's foreman knew all about her. 'She is the Moabitess who came back from Moab with Naomi,' he replied when Boaz asked him about her (v.6).

Naomi's return

The events leading up to Naomi's return to Bethlehem are played out in Act One. Naomi had previously lived in Bethlehem for many years, so she was well known by the community there. But when famine came, her husband, Elimelech, had taken her and their two sons, Mahlon and Kilion, to live in the nearby land of Moab, with whom Israel was at peace for a change.

The Moabites were descended from Lot (see Chapter 1), but were usually hostile to their distant relatives, the Israelites. During the early period of the judges, after the death of Othniel (see Chapter 5), Eglon, king of Moab, had invaded and oppressed the Israelites for eighteen years (see Chapter 9). Elimelech's situation must have been desperate for him to contemplate taking his family there. But they seem to have been accepted in Moab, because their sons married Moabite women, Ruth and Orpah respectively.

Then tragedy struck. Naomi's husband and sons all died, leaving her a widow in a foreign land with no one to care for her. Naomi decided to return home to Bethlehem, where she hoped to be able to beg food to live. The Law of Moses stipulated that the nearest male relative of the dead husband should look after the widow. Naomi had no such relative in Moab, and could only hope against hope that she had have a living relative back in Bethlehem.

Naomi urged her daughters-in-law to stay in Moab, where they could rebuild their lives. Orpah decided to stay, but Ruth insisted on accompanying her mother-in-law, saying, 'Don't urge me to leave you or to turn back from you. Where you go I will go, and where you stay I will stay. Your people will be my people and your God my God' (1:16). Ruth was prepared to leave her family, her culture, and everything she knew to look after Naomi. Quite how Ruth's parents reacted to their daughter's decision to leave them in preference for her mother-in-law, we can only imagine. And so, the two widows finally arrived in Bethlehem, where Naomi told the people of the town all that had befallen her since she left all those years ago.

Reputation

Not only was Boaz's foreman impressed by this foreign woman's loyalty and devotion to Naomi, but also by the fact that she had actually asked permission to glean in the field, and had worked tirelessly (v.7). Ruth was willing to work at such a menial task with all her heart, even though it was degrading and showed that she was the lowest of the low in the community. How do we react when we are asked to do something for God's kingdom that we consider to be beneath us? Do we feel insulted by what we've been called to do, and do it half-heartedly? Or do we feel honoured to be called to work for the Master in any capacity, and give it our very best? As Ruth was about to find out, such small opportunities often lead to something far greater (Matt. 25:21,23).

Having heard what his foreman said, Boaz himself was clearly impressed with this young woman, and went over to speak to her. Addressing her as 'daughter' (v.8) – which not only suggests that he was considerably older than her, but implied that he now regarded her as family rather than as a foreigner – Boaz insisted that she stayed in his field under his protection. True to his character, Boaz was doing what was right, because an unaccompanied woman gleaning in a field was in a very vulnerable position (v.22). Now Ruth could glean in safety, walking behind Boaz's servant girls, and could have a drink whenever she liked, knowing she wouldn't be molested (vv.8–9).

Ruth was overwhelmed by Boaz's sensitivity and kindness towards her, a foreigner, and asked him why he was treating her so well (v.10). Boaz replied that he had been told all about her (probably by his foreman) and how much he had been impressed by the self-sacrifice she had made for Naomi's sake (v.11). In recognition of this, Boaz then said, 'May the LORD repay you for what you have done. May you be richly rewarded by the LORD, the God of Israel, under whose wings you have come to take refuge' (v.12). True to her character, Ruth remained humble in the face of such favour, and thanked Boaz for being so kind to her, describing herself as a servant lower than his servant girls (v.13).

Ruth's good reputation went before her, and paved the way for her relationship with Boaz to develop. What sort of reputation do we have in our families, at work, with our neighbours? Is it the kind that will develop into an opportunity for us to share our faith with them? In my experience, a good reputation doesn't happen overnight. It has to be worked at daily, and seen to be consistent with what we believe, otherwise it will not ring true, and what we say will be dismissed. Let's be under no illusions: we are being watched.

Of all the fields ...

When the mealtime arrived, Boaz again paid special attention to Ruth. He made sure she was not only included, but also well fed and looked after (v.14). And when they all returned to work, Boaz instructed his workers to deliberately leave behind some stalks of grain from the bundles on the ground so Ruth could gather them (vv.15–16). In the way he treated Ruth, Boaz generously went way beyond what was required of him in the Law of Moses in providing for the poor. Are we as generous in our dealings with others, or are we satisfied with doing the bare minimum?

Boaz would have noticed how Ruth kept hard at it until evening, and then threshed the barley she'd gathered by hand, probably with a stick. It amounted to about twenty-two litres, equivalent to half a month's wages – a huge return for one day's gleaning. Was Boaz already thinking that Ruth was the sort of woman he'd been waiting for all his life? Of all the fields in all of Bethlehem, she had walked into his!

Naomi was absolutely thrilled when she saw the fruit of Ruth's labours, and couldn't wait to hear all the news (vv.17–19). When she found out that Ruth had been gleaning in one of Boaz's fields, Naomi was delighted. Naomi had already been impressed by Boaz's kindness to all and sundry in the Bethlehem area; but she had been particularly thrilled to discover that Boaz was 'a relative on her husband's side from the clan of Elimelech' (v.1). As she enthused to Ruth, 'That man is our close relative; he is one of our kinsman-redeemers' (v.20). A beam of hope had shone into their dark situation.

As it turned out

Ruth was obviously so excited and carried away by all that had happened to her, that she didn't even stop to ask Naomi what on earth a 'kinsman-redeemer' might be, but just carried on with her story of the day (v.21). Naomi, however, must have been very much aware of the future possibilities given that Boaz, their kinsman-redeemer, seemed to have taken a liking to Ruth. So Naomi encouraged Ruth to spend the rest of the spring harvest gleaning under the protection of Boaz (vv.22–23), presumably in the hope that he would become even more attracted to Ruth during the days ahead.

Did Naomi know about Boaz being her relative before Ruth went out to glean that first day, and subtly point her in the direction of the field where Boaz was harvesting? But then, did Naomi even know which fields belonged to Boaz? Or did she simply trust God to guide Ruth to the right field where she would meet Boaz? Ruth certainly didn't know whose field she was gleaning in. Whatever the truth of the matter, 'As it turned out, she found herself working in a field belonging to Boaz' (v.3).

This was surely no coincidence; God's hand was at work. God had brought together a rich landowner and an impoverished foreigner to fulfil His purposes. Isn't it amazing how, the more we pray and trust God to guide us, the more 'coincidences' – or should that be 'God-incidences' – seem to happen in our lives, so that His purposes might be fulfilled?

What a difference a night makes! (Ruth 3)
At the threshing floor

Act Three of the drama sees Boaz spending the night at the threshing floor. This was the place where the produce of the fields was brought by donkey or cart to be threshed and winnowed, a process which separated the precious grain from the stalks and the chaff. Boaz would have been there to stop any thieves from stealing his produce, and to wait his turn to thresh. What he didn't know was that a pair of eyes was watching his every move from the shadows, accompanied no doubt by a rapidly beating heart.

Naomi had been quite clear in her instructions. Perhaps disappointed that after all these weeks their kinsman Boaz had made no move towards marrying Ruth, whom she had come to regard as her own daughter, Naomi seems to have decided to help the situation along (3:1). 'Wash and perfume yourself, and put on your best clothes,' she had said to Ruth (v.3). Such preparations are reminiscent of those carried out by a bride (Ezek. 16:9–12). Ruth had dutifully obeyed, and made her way to the threshing floor as instructed.

As she waited there unobserved, hearing the laughter and noise of the threshers as they ate and drank together, Ruth must have been going over the rest of Naomi's strange instructions carefully in her mind: don't let Boaz know you are there; watch where he lies down to sleep; when he's asleep, go and uncover his feet, and lie down next to them as a servant would; when he finds you there, ask him to spread the corner of his garment over you, because he is a kinsman-redeemer.

Kinsman-redeemer

A 'kinsman-redeemer' was a male relative who was prepared voluntarily to protect and provide for the nearest relatives within his extended family who were destitute or in difficulty, and had no way of resolving their problems. This could involve him marrying a widow to produce an heir for her husband; redeeming land that a poor relative had sold outside the family; redeeming a relative who had been sold into slavery; even avenging the killing of a relative. He was not obliged to do any of these things, in which case, the opportunity would pass to the next nearest relative, and so on.

Ruth's problem was that she couldn't take advantage of the Levirate marriage system (Deut. 25:5–10), as Naomi had no other sons she could marry. In Israelite culture, a husband's inheritance was passed down to his son, not to his wife. So if she remained a widow, or took a husband from outside the family, Mahlon's inheritance would pass to his nearest male relative and Ruth would not benefit from it. Ruth's only hope was for a kinsman-redeemer to appear on the scene.

Praise God that a kinsman-redeemer has appeared on the scene to redeem us from the consequences of sin (Titus 2:11,14) – Jesus Christ, who came to buy us back with His own precious blood shed on the cross, thus assuring us of an eternal inheritance (Eph. 1:7,14; 1 Pet. 1:18–19). He wasn't obliged to come and save us, but He knew we were lost without Him. So out of His great grace, love and mercy Jesus came willingly and voluntarily to lay down His life for each one of us (John 10:11; Eph. 2:4–5).

Very strange

This Israelite provision of a kinsman-redeemer, and the customs that went with it, must have sounded very strange to Ruth as a foreigner in the land. But she was prepared to follow Naomi's instructions, because she respected her mother-in-law's wisdom and integrity, and knew Naomi only wanted the best for her.

How we should thank God for people like these in our families and churches: wise men and women of integrity, with experience of life, to whom we can turn for advice, help and prayer support! But do we actually turn to them for help, or are we too proud? And when they give us advice, do we actually listen to it, or do we always think we know better?

A startling discovery

The evening festivities over, Boaz went to lie down at the far end of the threshing floor. Ruth must have been relieved at this, for it would at least afford them a modicum of privacy. Boaz soon fell fast asleep, only to be startled awake in the middle of the night – to make an even more startling discovery (v.8). Perhaps he thought he could smell perfume ... then, on raising himself up, he saw a woman lying at his feet.

Boaz, a man of high moral standing, must have been shocked to find himself in such a compromising situation. When Ruth identified herself, asked for the corner of his garment to cover her, and told him that he was a kinsman-redeemer, Boaz realised immediately what was going on. Ruth wasn't trying to seduce him; she was submissively making a proposal of marriage in the only way open to her (Ezek. 16:8).

Boaz responded genuinely and without hesitation. Far from rejecting her, as Ruth knew Boaz had every right to do, he again called her 'daughter' (v.10). Boaz went on to comment on her kindness to Naomi, whom he knew Ruth was keen to provide for. He commended Ruth for not seeking a husband outside Naomi's extended family, but being willing to observe the Israelite custom, even though that meant she would have to marry a much older man.

Boaz was prepared to do what was right in this situation, as Naomi undoubtedly knew he would. Boaz confirmed that he was able and willing to do all Ruth was asking of him, and could do so with the full support of the Bethlehem community, who had all been impressed by Ruth's 'noble character' (v.11). But, as Boaz went on to explain, there was a problem: 'there is a kinsman-redeemer nearer than I' (v.12).

First refusal

Clearly, Boaz had been thinking about the matter and, although he was prepared to marry Ruth, he was also a man who did things by the book. Whatever his personal feelings were at this point, Boaz knew that this other kinsman was entitled to first refusal. Boaz told Ruth that the matter would be sorted out in the morning, and swore to her that if the other party was not willing, 'as surely as the LORD lives I will do it' (v.13).

Perhaps as a confirmation of his intent, Boaz insisted that Ruth lay at his feet until morning. Ruth left at first light, but not before Boaz had loaded her up with as much barley as she could carry. Keen to protect his and Ruth's reputation, Boaz said, 'Don't let it be known that a woman came to the threshing-floor' (v.14). To whom Boaz addressed these words is not clear. It could have been to Ruth herself; or was it to the other threshers who had also spent the night on the floor?

Naomi was all agog to hear how everything had gone! When Ruth had finished her account of the night's events, Naomi expressed her confidence that Boaz was a man of his word. Can people we know express such faith in our integrity? Like Boaz, do we stand out as people who are true to our word, reliable and can be trusted? Are we seen as people of honour and discretion, who do what is right?

At the town gate (Ruth 4)
The case is heard

Act Four opens with Boaz going to the town gate. This was the place where the elders of the town would sit to discuss council matters, make business transactions, and hold a court of law. The walls afforded shade, and the people of the town would sit around on the seats provided talking, watching and hearing all that was taking place.

Boaz knew that the kinsman he was looking for was bound to come this way sooner or later and, sure enough, he did. Boaz called him over, sat him down, and gathered together ten of the town's elders with them, thus constituting a court of law. He then laid out the case very astutely and cleverly. Boaz explained that there was a property issue to be decided. Elimelech, Naomi's husband, had owned land in the area. But when they had gone to Moab, someone else would have cultivated and harvested it. Now that the harvest was over, it was the right time for the land to be sold. Boaz told the kinsman that, as Naomi wanted to keep the land in the family, she was giving him first refusal. If he wasn't interested in redeeming the land, then Boaz confirmed that he himself was willing to buy it back as the next nearest relative.

When the kinsman said, 'I will redeem it' (4:4), Boaz went on to explain how there was more to this matter than might at first be apparent. Elimelech had the right to an heir who would inherit his estate. Since Elimelech's daughter-in-law, Ruth, was still living, whoever bought the land would have to marry Ruth in order to provide an heir for Elimelech. The land would automatically belong to any son Ruth had, so the kinsman would lose the land he had bought, and have a second family to maintain at the same time.

Too much

The thought of this was too much for the kinsman, who was probably already married with a family. He replied, 'Then I cannot redeem it because I might endanger my own estate. You redeem it yourself. I cannot do it' (v.6). As the kinsman found out, the right choice is often not the easy choice, and the easy choice is often not the right choice. Like the kinsman, are we inclined to make the easy choice rather than the right choice?

Boaz had got what he wanted. As was the custom, the agreement was sealed by the kinsman giving one of his sandals to Boaz. Boaz then announced to the elders and the townsfolk that they were witnesses to the business that had been transacted regarding Elimelech's field, and to the fact that he had acquired Ruth as his wife (vv.8–10). The townspeople rejoiced, and bestowed their blessings on Boaz and Ruth's future together. They mentioned Perez, the son of Judah and Tamar, in their good wishes. Not only was Perez an ancestor of Boaz, but he had been born as a result of Judah not giving his daughter-in-law Tamar her rights with regard to Levirate marriage (see Chapter 4). In contrast to Judah, Boaz was prepared to do what was right by Naomi and Ruth.

Marriage and after

And so Boaz, the son of the Canaanite woman Rahab, the prostitute from Jericho (see Chapter 7), was married to Ruth, the daughter of a Moabite, an enemy of Israel. Which just goes to show that it's not our background that God is concerned about – it's our hearts and minds that matter to Him (Mark 12:30).

A relationship that began purely as a matter of family business seems to have developed into a deep love. Boaz and Ruth had a son called Obed, a shortened form of Obadiah, which means 'servant of the Lord', which obviously summed up their hopes for him. The women of Bethlehem rejoiced for Naomi, who had a grandson at last, and a kinsman-redeemer to look after her and protect her; not to mention a daughter-in-law who, in the words of the women, 'loves you and who is better to you than seven sons' (v.15).

What a lovely picture is portrayed by the words, 'Then Naomi took the child, laid him in her lap and cared for him' (v.16). After all she had been through, Naomi could now rest in the knowledge that her husband's name would continue, and his land in Bethlehem would have an heir, thanks to the generosity of Boaz.

It seems likely that Obed stayed in the Bethlehem area, where he had a son named Jesse, the father of David. Was it in Elimelech's field that David composed his songs as he looked after the family sheep, and saw off the lion and the bear? Boaz and Ruth would be the great-grandparents of the greatest of all Israel's kings, and ancestors of the King of kings (Matt. 1:5).

Chapter 13

Effective and Ineffective

Eli

**1 Samuel 1:9–18,25–28; 2:12–17;
2:22–3:21; 4:1–21**
(Other bit part players appearing: Elkanah, Hophni, Phinehas)

Eli the priest (1 Samuel 1:9–18,25–28)
The tabernacle at Shiloh

Eli was the high priest at Shiloh, which by this time had become the religious centre of the nation. The main sanctuary, the tabernacle, is variously referred to as 'the house of the LORD', 'the LORD's temple', 'the Tent of Meeting', and 'my dwelling' (1:7,9; 2:22,32). There are also references to sleeping quarters and doors (3:2,15), all of which indicates that the tabernacle had by now become part of a larger, more permanent structure which could justifiably be described as a 'temple'.

It seems likely that Eli was a descendant of Ithamar, the youngest son of Aaron. He was both judge and high priest of Israel, and was approaching forty years of service to God at the time of these events. All the priests wore an ephod, which was a plain linen sleeveless vest. By contrast, the ephod worn by Eli as high priest was bright and rich with colour. Part of this special ephod was a breastpiece with twelve precious stones attached: one for each of the tribes of Israel. The breastpiece also contained a pouch, within which were the Urim and Thummim – two small, flat objects used for discerning God's will (Exod. 28:6–30).

Enter Hannah

Eli must have seen Hannah many times before, but never like this. She had been coming annually to Shiloh for many years with her husband and the family to worship and offer sacrifices (1:3–5); but never before had she come into the sanctuary alone. Eli could tell that she was preoccupied, because she didn't seem to see him sitting there at the entrance as she came in. Then he heard her weeping, and saw that her mouth was moving, but no words were forthcoming. Eli jumped to the conclusion that Hannah must have had a bit too much to drink, and probably stood there watching her while bemoaning the fact that people nowadays didn't treat the sanctuary with the respect that they should.

Annoyed, Eli went up to Hannah and asked tersely, 'How long will you keep on getting drunk? Get rid of your wine' (v.14). Hannah was shocked to hear the high priest's accusation, and assured him that she was perfectly sober. Hannah went on to explain to Eli that she was in such deep anguish that she had felt the need to come into the sanctuary to pour out her heart to God.

The elderly Eli, with all his priestly perception and experience, immediately realised that Hannah was telling him the truth, and was clearly moved in his spirit by her distress. From being annoyed by her, Eli became completely supportive of her. Then and there he gently prayed for Hannah from the bottom of his heart: 'Go in peace, and may the God of Israel grant you what you have asked of him' (v.17).

How good are we at supporting other people in prayer when

they are in distress? Do we get alongside them, or do we pass them by? Sometimes it's hard to know what to pray for people in their despair. In my experience, praying for the person in languages inspired by the Spirit of God is probably the best thing to do at such times. An arm round the shoulder, or a hug, can also convey our support without a word needing to be said.

Three years later

When Hannah left the Temple, it was the last time that Eli would see her for at least three years. Then, one day, there in the sanctuary, he looked up and saw Hannah coming towards him with her husband, Elkanah – and with a little boy holding her by the hand. What emotions must have welled up within Eli as Hannah said to him, 'As surely as you live, my lord, I am the woman who stood here beside you praying to the LORD. I prayed for this child, and the LORD has granted me what I asked of him. So now I give him to the LORD. For his whole life he shall be given over to the LORD' (vv.26–28).

Eli seems to have accepted Hannah's decision without question. This suggests that Eli knew this was God's doing, and was willing to take on the responsibility of looking after, and bringing up, a very young boy. Training Samuel up to be a priest wouldn't have been a problem, but as for his day-to-day upbringing – that was some commitment for an old man to take on! Presumably he got help with this from some of the local women.

Are we as willing as Eli was to submit ourselves to God's will, to the extent of taking on responsibilities we don't really feel equipped for, or think God could have given to others? But has God not promised to 'equip you with everything good for doing his will' (Heb. 13:21)?

Eli the father (1 Samuel 2:12-17,22-26)
Sinning sons

Although Eli was undoubtedly effective as a priest, he was patently ineffective as a father. His two sons, Hophni and Phinehas, were persistently behaving in a disreputable way, but Eli did little to correct them: 'Eli's sons were wicked men; they had no regard for the LORD' (2:12). In Hebrew, the phrase 'had no regard for' literally means 'did not know'. Throughout the Old Testament, knowing God is not just intellectual – it is spiritual. It means being in close fellowship with God, and having a personal relationship with Him.

Although Hophni and Phinehas served as priests in the sanctuary (1:3), they appear to have had no such relationship with God. Unlike their father Eli, who was a godly man and took his priestly responsibilities very seriously, Hophni and Phinehas were ungodly men who took their duties as priests flippantly, preferring to take advantage of their position for their own selfish ends. Their greed and arrogance was breathtaking, and was doing serious damage to the reputation and standing of the priesthood in Israel.

Not content with the provision made for them as priests by the Law of Moses through the tithing system (Num. 18:20-24; Josh. 13:14,33), Eli's sons flagrantly abused the rules concerning the priests' portion of the fellowship offerings, made by the people at the sanctuary, to get more than their fair share of the meat (vv.13-16). They had no compunction about resorting to force if the people wouldn't comply with their demands. They were even taking their unfair share of the meat before it was offered to God on the altar, in direct contravention of the procedure laid down (Lev. 3:3-5). Thus Hophni and Phinehas were sinning by treating with utter contempt the offerings brought by the people to honour God and ask His forgiveness (v.17).

Besides acting in this disreputable way in the sanctuary, Hophni and Phinehas were also guilty of sexual immorality: 'they slept with the women who served at the entrance to the Tent of

Meeting' (v.22). The way they flaunted their sinfulness suggests that they felt themselves to be untouchable.

Parental discipline

It's not as though Eli didn't know about his sons' scandalous behaviour, both in the sanctuary and out of it. The people bent his ear about it all the time. It must have been very wearisome for a man of his advanced years to be constantly bombarded about his sons' outrageous actions. In the end, Eli felt he had to try one more time (vv.23–25). He warned his sons about the inevitable consequences if they continued to sin against God; but they completely ignored him, and probably went away laughing at the old man's inability to discipline them.

This situation must have been the result of Eli's constant failure down the years to correct his sons' behaviour. He had clearly lacked the necessary determination and resolve to discipline them from a young age. Eli's words of rebuke had obviously not been followed up by any effective sanctions to reform their behaviour, so his discipline was ineffective. Hophni and Phinehas grew up ignoring him and doing their own thing. Eli continued to feebly plead with them to mend their ways, but it was too late.

Eli had been an excellent example to his sons as to how a priest should conduct himself and relate to the people. Hophni and Phinehas knew very well what was required of them in their priestly office, but instead they chose to abuse their position of authority and trust, and to wilfully disobey God's commands. In the end, God's anger was such that he decided to 'put them to death' (v.25). God was not prepared to allow one of Eli's sons to become high priest in succession to him. Meanwhile Samuel, in sharp contrast to Hophni and Phinehas, 'continued to grow in stature and in favour with the LORD and with men' (v.26).

Eli's ineffectiveness as a parent raises some important questions for us. Are we prepared to discipline our children from their earliest years, or do we just let them do as they please? Many studies have shown how crucial the first five years of a child's life are; there the foundations are laid for the rest of their upbringing. Being an example is essential, but it's not enough. Unlike Eli, do we have the determination to back up our words with appropriate and effective sanctions? We all know how wilful children, and particularly teenagers, can be, which makes disciplining them a tough undertaking. But in my experience it is vital for their welfare and development. Admittedly, even well-disciplined children can go off the rails; but at least the parents know before God that they did everything they could to obey the command, 'Train a child in the way he should go' (Prov. 22:6).

The Bible also tells us that 'the Lord disciplines those he loves ... God disciplines us for our good' (Heb. 12:6,10). How good are we at responding positively to God's discipline in our lives? Like Samuel, do we accept it, rejoice in it, and become more mature because of it? Or, like Hophni and Phinehas, do we reject it, resent it, and become more immature as a result?

God speaks (1 Samuel 2:27-3:21)
A matter of honour

Shortly after Eli's latest display of ineffectiveness, a prophet, or 'man of God' (2:27) came to see him. Through this unnamed prophet, God was going to leave Eli in no doubt as to what was about to happen to the priesthood in Israel as a result of Eli's failure to discharge his responsibilities properly.

The prophet began by reminding Eli of his priestly heritage, going all the way back to Aaron. Then he went on to make it clear that Eli was guilty of complicity with his sons in their sins as priests, because he had ignored their wrongdoing and let them carry on unchecked (vv.28–29). The high priest was obliged to take the strongest possible action against any priest who stepped out of line (Num. 15:22–31). The least Eli should have done was remove them from their priestly office.

Eli had clearly failed to confront his sons and stop their sinful behaviour. Indeed, he had honoured them above God, and had become fat through eating his fill of the meat they had illegally obtained from the peoples' sacrifices (4:18). God was displeased with Eli's complicity, and said to him through the prophet, 'Why do you honour your sons more than me by fattening yourselves on the choice parts of every offering made by my people Israel? ... Those who honour me I will honour, but those who despise me will be disdained' (vv.29–30). Eli and his sons had failed to honour God, and there were to be drastic consequences.

Is there something in our close family that has been allowed to go on for years, even though we know it to be wrong? Are we willing to acknowledge that we have been at least partly responsible for this by doing nothing, and ask God for the boldness and courage to confront the situation?

Isn't it encouraging to know that, if we seek to honour God in our lives in all we say and do, He will honour us in return? Is there anyone or anything in our lives that we are honouring above God at the moment? If so, are we aware that this could have serious repercussions for us? Isn't it better to restore God to His rightful place, and honour Him above all?

God's judgment

The prophet then announced God's judgment on Eli's family (vv.31–36). Hophni and Phinehas would both be cut off in their prime and die on the same day (v.34). The rest of Eli's family would be reduced to begging for employment in lowly priestly offices to survive (v.36). The prediction that 'there will not be an old man in your family line' (v.31) not only foretold the death of his sons, but also the future massacre of his descendants by King Saul at Nob (22:18–19), and the removal of Abiathar from the priesthood by King Solomon, marking the end of Eli's line (1 Kings 2:26–27).

Abiathar would be replaced by Zadok, thus fulfilling the prophecy given here that 'I will raise up for myself a faithful priest, who will do according to what is in my heart and mind. I will firmly establish his house, and he will minister before my anointed one [the king] always' (v.35). Zadok was a priest in King David's time, and then appointed high priest under King Solomon. Zadok's priestly line remained in place probably until the time of Ezra.

The death of Eli's sons would be a sign to him that all these other predictions would come to pass as well. God also said that there would be 'distress in my dwelling' (v.32). This would include the capture of the ark of God, the destruction of Shiloh, and the transfer of the tabernacle elsewhere. Eli would live to see the ark being captured by the Philistines. The destruction of Shiloh probably took place in the aftermath of the battle in which the ark was lost. The actual moving of the tabernacle to Nob would happen after Eli's death (21:1–6).

Interestingly, there was nothing in this prophecy about the future of Samuel. He was not the 'faithful priest' referred to, nor was his family 'firmly establish[ed]' as priests. In any case, Samuel didn't qualify for becoming the next high priest, as he was not descended from Aaron. Samuel's role was going to be that of judge, and most importantly, of prophet, who would bring the word of the Lord once more to Israel after a long period of absence during the time of the judges. The prophetic aspect of Samuel's future ministry was about to begin in a rather dramatic way.

'Here I am'

By now, Samuel was probably about twelve years old. 'In those days the word of the LORD was rare; there were not many visions' (3:1). These two types of prophetic gifts were now uncommon. There had only been two prophets and five revelations during the 300-year period of the judges. Israel was in desperate need of prophetic guidance, but few seemed willing to listen to God. No wonder Eli was slow to realise that it was God who was speaking to Samuel.

Samuel didn't know what to make of it either. Understandably, when he heard the voice speaking to him, Samuel thought it was Eli calling. Since Eli was virtually blind by now, Samuel must have thought the high priest was summoning him for help. Samuel probably slept with the other priests in one of the small rooms just outside the Holy Place, which was situated in front of the Most Holy Place where the ark of God was kept.

This touching night-time scene occurred three times. On each occasion, the voice called him by name, and Samuel ran to where Eli lay asleep, saying, 'Here I am; you called me' (vv.5–6,8). It seems that Eli had become very fond of Samuel, calling him 'My son' (v.6). Eli probably wished with all his heart that Samuel was his son, rather than those two revolting rogues he couldn't control. Twice Eli told Samuel that he hadn't called him. But then, on the third occasion, he suddenly realised what might be happening, and instructed Samuel accordingly: 'Go and lie down, and if he calls you, say, "Speak, LORD, for your servant is listening"' (v.9).

When God speaks to us through His Word, through a sermon, through the gifts of the Spirit, or some other way, are we willing to listen to His voice? And, having listened, is our response the same as that of Isaiah when the Lord spoke to him: 'Here am I. Send me' (Isa. 6:8)? Or are we more inclined to answer as Moses did initially: 'O Lord, please send someone else to do it' (Exod. 4:13)? May God give us all the grace to respond positively to His call.

Confirmation

The message God gave to Samuel confirmed the prophecy spoken previously by the unnamed prophet. Eli was guilty before God, not because he was 'contemptible' like his sons, but because 'he failed to restrain them' (v.13). In my experience, it's very easy to become so engrossed in the work of God, as Eli undoubtedly did, that we forget to pay proper attention to our family responsibilities. This must be a particularly difficult balance to strike for those in full-time ministry. Even Samuel would have problems in this area with his own two sons, Joel and Abijah, with heartbreaking consequences (8:1–3). Eli's experience emphasises how important it is to God that we seek to bring up our families in a way that is pleasing to Him.

No wonder Samuel kept quiet about what God had told him! He was afraid to tell Eli, and probably didn't want to hurt the feelings of the old man who had looked after him so kindly these past nine or so years. In the end, Eli dragged the truth out of the reluctant boy. On hearing this confirmation of God's judgment, Eli resigned himself to his fate: 'He is the LORD; let him do what is good in his eyes' (v.18). At least Eli had the grace to accept that he and his family deserved all that was coming to them, acknowledging that God's justice is perfect.

From Eli's point of view, Samuel was probably an unexpected person for God to use to bring him this message. And isn't it true that God often uses unexpected channels in the work of His kingdom? How many times have we been surprised by who God has used to minister into a particular situation, or by the way it has been done? So doesn't that mean that we can all expect to be used by God in unexpected ways? The question is, are we willing to be so used? Isn't it exciting to serve a God with whom we can always expect the unexpected?

Disaster strikes (1 Samuel 4:1–21)
Fetch the ark!

Eli must have wondered how and why his sons would both die on the same day. He was about to find out. Their neighbours the Philistines attacked in force, and the Israelites went out to fight them, sustaining heavy losses (4:2). When this news reached the ears of the Israelite elders, they met to discuss why the Lord had brought this defeat upon them. They decided to fetch the ark of God from Shiloh 'so that it may go with us and save us from the hand of our enemies' (v.3). The elders had failed to grasp the real reason for the defeat.

The ark of God, also known as the ark of the covenant, was a powerful symbol of the presence of God. In it were contained the ten commandments given to Moses by God. Not surprisingly, Hophni and Phinehas had no compunction about entering the

Most Holy Place to remove the ark, even though only the high priest was supposed to go in there, and then only once a year on the Day of Atonement. To their minds, there was a matter to be dealt with that was far more important than worrying about desecrating a holy place.

Once again, Eli appears to have done nothing to stop Hophni and Phinehas. They and the rest of the Israelites had come to believe that the ark itself was their source of power, not God. Eli seems to have made no attempt to explain to the elders that God would not grant them victory because they had gone away from Him as a nation.

Big mistake

The people were making the big mistake of thinking that, if they took the ark into battle, they were taking God's power and presence with them, and nothing could stand against them. They were almost using it like a lucky charm, or an idol. Its arrival in the camp certainly raised the spirits of the soldiers, who mistakenly thought they were now bound to be victorious (v.5).

In the event, they were slaughtered, losing 30,000 foot soldiers. Hophni and Phinehas, who had carried the ark into battle, were also killed, and the ark was captured by the Philistines (vv.10–11). As far as the Israelites were concerned, that meant God's power, presence and glory had gone from Israel – God had deserted them. When she heard the news, Phinehas' wife went into labour, and named her son Ichabod, which means 'no glory', saying, 'The glory has departed from Israel' (v.21).

The death of Eli

All Eli could do was sit on his chair by the side of the road at the entrance to Shiloh waiting for news. The fact that 'his heart feared for the ark of God' (v.13) seems to suggest that Eli was against them taking the ark into battle, but could do nothing to stop them. Due to his blindness, he didn't see the Benjamite messenger who had run from the battlefield. The Benjamite's clothes were torn and there was dust on his head: symbols that he brought bad news (v.12).

Eli was suddenly aware of uproar around him, and asked what was going on (v.14). The Benjamite told Eli the news that his sons had been killed, and the ark had been captured (vv.16–17). When the messenger mentioned the ark, Eli 'fell backwards off his chair by the side of the gate. His neck was broken and he died, for he was an old man and heavy' (v.18). It was the news about the ark of God, rather than of his sons' death, that shocked Eli to the core and caused him to fall awkwardly and break his neck. Eli seems to have been more concerned about the fate of the ark than the fate of his sons.

Eli was ninety-eight years old when he died, and had led Israel for forty years (vv.15,18). Blind, not only physically, but also to the sins of his sons and the degeneracy of Israel, Eli died a sorry, even tragic, figure. His death marked the end of an era. Israel was now at a nadir, symbolised by the ark of God being in the possession of the Philistines. It would take an exceptional leader to drag them back up again. God's plan for Samuel was about to come to fruition.

Chapter 14

Bittersweet Love

Michal

1 Samuel 18; 19:11–17; 2 Samuel 3:12–16; 6:12–23
(Other bit part players appearing: Ish-Bosheth, Abner, Paltiel)

The used daughter (1 Samuel 18)
Love sweet love

Princess Michal, the younger daughter of King Saul and his wife Ahinoam, had fallen head over heels in love with the nation's handsome hero, David. After his slaying of Goliath, David had become part of Saul's court (17:1–58). Over the next few years, 'Whatever Saul sent him to do, David did it so successfully that Saul gave him a high rank in the army. This pleased all the people, and Saul's officers as well' (18:5). But as David became increasingly successful, Saul became increasingly jealous, and tried to kill him twice (vv.10–11). This must have horrified Michal and also her brother, Jonathan, who had formed a deep bond of friendship with David (v.3).

But what probably horrified Michal even more was her father's plan to marry David to her older sister, Merab. And there was absolutely nothing she could do about it. The prospect of seeing the object of her love in the arms of another woman, especially her sister, must have been difficult for Michal to bear. Actually, Saul was only doing this as part of his strategy, borne of his insane jealousy, to get rid of David. His marriage terms of lifetime military service would result in David's death in battle sooner or later, Saul reasoned. When David protested that he was not worthy to become the son-in-law of the king, Saul married Merab off to someone else (vv.17–19). Michal must have been overwhelmed with joy at her father's decision. She was back in with a chance!

An unusual dowry

When Saul found out that Michal was in love with David, he decided to use his daughter to trap David into agreeing to his revised but still unreasonable marriage terms. Saul even got his servants to persuade David that becoming the king's son-in-law would be a good move. This time, Saul's marriage terms were not lifetime service, but 'a hundred Philistine foreskins' (v.25) – a rather unusual dowry to say the least! Not that Saul thought David had any chance of achieving this; he was sure that David would die in the attempt, thus getting rid of the object of his jealousy in a way that would attach no blame to him at all.

Did Michal realise what her father was actually up to in demanding such a dowry? Her heart must have been in her mouth as David and his men set off to attack the Philistines. Would she ever see him alive again? She must have been on tenterhooks all the time David was gone, gazing into the distance in the hope of glimpsing his return. What jubilation and excitement she must have felt when David and his men finally came back having killed twice as many Philistines as Saul had required. My hero! Now she could get on with planning the wedding. Every young woman in the land would be envious of her marrying the nation's 'pin-up' boy!

It's easy to condemn Saul for his actions, but are we ever tempted to use other people for our own purposes, even members of our close family? Do we ever try to manipulate situations for our own selfish ends, like Saul did? If so, do we not stand condemned along with Saul? He never did repent. Have we?

The resourceful wife (1 Samuel 19:11–17)
Escape into the night

Michal and David were duly married, and lived in their own house. But even though his plan had spectacularly backfired, Saul was still determined to be rid of David. One evening, Saul sent his men to David's house to keep watch and to kill him in the morning (v.11).

Seeing her father's men outside, and realising what was going to happen, Michal took the initiative. She told David that he must escape under the cover of darkness, or he was a dead man (v.11). So Michal 'let David down through a window' (v.12), presumably by means of knotted bed sheets, and he fled into the darkness. What conflicting emotions she must have felt: an overwhelming determination to protect David and get him to safety, along with deep anguish at their parting, wondering when she would see him again. In fact, it would only be after the deaths of her father Saul and her brother Jonathan that she would meet David once more, and under very strange and highly emotional circumstances.

Cool under pressure

With David safely gone, Michal must have sat down and thought what to do next. What could she say to her father's men when they came banging on the door in the morning that would buy David more time to get further away from danger? Then she had an idea. Taking an idol, she dressed it in one of David's robes. Then, as a final touch, she got some goat's hair and adorned the head of the idol with it. She put the idol on their bed, and waited for morning (v.13).

The inevitable knock on the door duly came, and Michal let Saul's men in. Remaining cool and calm, she told them her deliberate lie: 'He is ill' (v.14). Presumably the men went into the bedroom, and saw the figure lying there, which they must have assumed was David. They reported this back to Saul, who wasn't the slightest bit interested in whether David was ill or not. 'Bring him up to me in his bed so that I may kill him', Saul instructed them, angrily (v.15).

On their return, the men found that it wasn't David in the bed at all (v.16). Saul must have been absolutely furious at this news, and stormed off to confront Michal. 'Why did you deceive me like this and send my enemy away so that he escaped?' he demanded of his daughter. Michal lied again, making out that David threatened to kill her if she tried to stop him escaping (v.17).

This episode raises the thorny question of whether it is ever acceptable to tell lies. The Bible clearly teaches that deliberately deceiving other people, or bearing false witness against them, is not right (Exod. 20:16; Col. 3:9). But what about matters of life and death, where to tell a lie is to save someone's life? Corrie ten Boom found herself in just such a situation when she was hiding Jews from the Nazis in her house in Holland. When a Nazi officer asked her outright where the Jews were hiding, she replied that there were no Jews in the house. Presumably she did this on the grounds that she was protecting peoples' lives, and could not bring herself to give them up to be killed. If we're honest, most of us would do exactly the same in such a situation, particularly to protect someone we love. So, does it come down to the circumstances and the conscience of the individual before God? Or should the letter of the law be applied in all situations, irrespective of any other considerations?

This incident was to have serious repercussions for Michal. Some time later, Saul married her off to a man called Paltiel. It's not clear whether this was done out of revenge for his daughter's lies, or out of spitefulness, or as a sign that he was cutting off every link his family had with David, or for some other reason. Whether Michal had any affection at all for Paltiel is not known, but he loved her deeply, as we shall see.

The political wife (2 Samuel 3:12-16)
Used again

Michal's father Saul, and her brothers Abinadab, Malki-Shua and Jonathan, were all killed in the same battle against the Philistines at Mount Gilboa (see 1 Sam. 31). Michal must have been totally devastated over the death of her brothers, if not the demise of her father. David was subsequently anointed king over the southern tribes of Judah, while the northern tribes of Israel made Ish-Bosheth, one of Saul's sons, their king. Ish-Bosheth was a weak king, who was dominated by Abner, his chief military leader. Abner offered to negotiate peace with David, and to bring the northern tribes over to him.

Before he would even contemplate this, David demanded that Abner return his wife Michal to him. By this time, David had several wives, so why did he insist on Michal being restored to him? Probably because he wanted to demonstrate to the whole of Israel that he was still married to a daughter of Saul. This would strengthen his claim to the throne of Israel, and show that he bore no grudges against the descendants of Saul. Michal was about to be used again.

David didn't wait for Abner to act; he sent his own messengers direct to Ish-Bosheth demanding in no uncertain terms: 'Give me my wife Michal, whom I betrothed to myself for the price of a hundred Philistine foreskins' (2 Sam. 3:14). Ish-Bosheth complied immediately, and gave orders that Michal be taken away from her husband, Paltiel, and sent back to David.

Helpless

How did Michal feel when she heard what was going to happen to her? She seems to have settled down well with Paltiel, who was totally devoted to her. With Paltiel, Michal had at least experienced some calm and normality in her life after the turbulence of being with David. But was she excited at the thought of returning to her first love, or was she no longer besotted with David?

Michal must have known that she would now be only one of

David's many wives; it wasn't going to be like the old days when she was the only one. She was about to be torn from the arms of a man who truly loved her exclusively with all his heart, to be thrust into a situation where she would be lonely, and David would have little time for her. Michal must have also known that her return was merely for political expediency, and not because David was yearning for her to be with him. One thing was for sure – she was helpless to do anything about the situation, even if she wanted to.

Michal's emotions at being parted from her husband are not recorded, but Paltiel's are: 'Her husband ... went with her, weeping behind her all the way to Bahurim' (v.16), the last place on the way to David's capital city of Hebron. He only went home when Abner shouted at him to do so.

Paltiel cuts a very sad and tragic figure: a victim initially of Saul's paranoia about David, and ultimately of David's political aims. He must have been a broken man but, like Michal, he was powerless to do anything to prevent her being taken away. Paltiel had no alternative but to return to his empty home and try to put the pieces of his life back together as best he could.

How many times has the equilibrium of our lives been upset by events over which we have no control? Suddenly, our world is shattered, and we feel broken apart. At such devastating times, let's recall the words of Isaiah, who wrote prophetically about Jesus: 'He has sent me to bind up the broken-hearted' (61:1), and also the words of the psalmists: 'God is our refuge and strength, an ever-present help in trouble'; '[The LORD] ... heals the broken-hearted and binds up their wounds' (46:1; 147:3). Isn't it comforting to know that, whatever we have to face, God is always there to minister to us?

It is interesting that never once throughout the whole of Michal's life is it recorded that she turned to God in her distress, or had any relationship with Him at all. She never experienced the help and healing in her life that was available to her. How sad it would be if we were to make the same mistake in our lives.

This incident also shows the far-reaching consequences that

jealousy and paranoia can have. Their tentacles enmesh not only those closest to the situation, but others who are innocent bystanders, such as Paltiel, causing misery, upset and distress. Isn't that all the more reason to nip such feelings in the bud before they create havoc?

The bitter wife (2 Samuel 6:12–23; *see also 1 Chronicles 15:25–29*)
Disgraceful exhibition

David eventually became king over Israel as well as Judah, thus unifying the nation once again. He went on to conquer Jerusalem, and he inflicted a crushing defeat on the Philistines. David made Jerusalem the capital city, and brought the ark of God there amidst scenes of great rejoicing. People were shouting, trumpets were sounding, choirs were singing, cymbals were crashing, harps and lyres were playing, and rams' horns were being blown loudly.

David was wearing an ephod made of fine linen, the garment of a priest (see Chapter 13), rather than his royal robes. All the Levites who were carrying the ark were also wearing fine linen ephods. David himself was leading the joyful celebrations with ecstatic abandon, and 'danced before the LORD with all his might' (6:14).

Michal was watching the procession from a window. When she saw David's behaviour, she was shocked, and 'despised him in her heart' (v.16). 'What a disgraceful exhibition he's making of himself, behaving in that totally undignified manner,' Michal must have thought. And she wasn't prepared to keep her thoughts to herself either! So, when David was on his way back home from making all the required sacrifices, and distributing food to the crowd, Michal went out to meet him.

If David was expecting expressions of joy and support from his wife at what had occurred, he was very much mistaken. Clearly, Michal was still seething about the way he had conducted himself, and said sarcastically, 'How the king of Israel has distinguished himself today, disrobing in the sight of the slave girls of his servants as any vulgar fellow would' (v.20).

Michal couldn't cope with such a display of expressive worship from her husband. Certainly, it was unconventional to worship in such a way at that time, but David made it plain to her that she 'ain't seen nothing yet!' (vv.21–22) Are we prone to criticise people who worship differently from us? Do we think that the way we do it is the only way to praise God? It seems to me that what matters to God is not how we worship, but whether we worship Him 'in spirit and in truth' (John 4:24).

Dealing

Interestingly, Michal is referred to as the 'daughter of Saul' (v.16) rather than as David's wife. This serves to emphasise her growing contempt for and bitterness towards David, which may well have started when he tore her away from Paltiel. Michal had now reached the stage where she loathed David for loving God. The consequence of all this was that 'Michal [the] daughter of Saul had no children to the day of her death' (v.23).

It's not hard to understand why Michal had become so bitter. All her life she was subject to circumstances beyond her control. She was used by her father for his own ends; her first love had to run off and leave her behind; then she was married off to a man she didn't know and, initially at least, didn't care for; and just when she was enjoying a secure, loving relationship, it was snatched away from her. Back in David's household, she must have felt unwanted and unloved. Besides which, she had no children, and never would have.

Michal serves as a warning to us all of what we can become if we allow bitterness to take root within us. That's why we are urged to 'Get rid of all bitterness' (Eph. 4:31). God warns us to be drastic with such feelings, and not give them room to grow. In my experience, this is far from easy, but God will enable us to deal with them as we commit our situations to Him.

We are all subject to circumstances beyond our control. It's how we respond to them that counts. To put it another way: it's not a matter of what life has dealt us, it's how we deal with what we've been dealt that matters.

Chapter 15

The Cold-blooded Commander

Joab

2 Samuel 2–5; 11; 13–20; 1 Kings 1:5–2:34
(Other bit part players appearing: Abner, Abishai, Asahel, Uriah,
Nathan, Absalom, Amasa, Adonijah, Benaiah)

David becomes king of Israel (2 Samuel 2–5)
Clash of the champions

After the death of Saul, David had been crowned king of Judah, and lived in Hebron, ruling the south of the country from there. Meanwhile, Abner, the commander of Saul's army, had made Ish-Bosheth, the son of Saul, king over the north of the country. Ish-Bosheth was a very weak king, and Abner was very much the power behind the throne. This division of Israel caused considerable tension between the two camps, and confrontations were inevitable.

The leader of David's army was Joab, one of three sons born to Zeruiah, the half-sister of David. So Joab was David's nephew. Realising that Joab and his men were moving northwards, claiming more territory as they went, Abner moved to cut off their advance. The two sides faced each other at the pool of Gibeon (2:13). Instead of engaging in battle, Abner proposed a clash of the champions, whereby twelve men from each side would be selected to fight their opposite number to the death. The side with the most champions left standing would be declared the winner. Joab agreed, and the contest began. At the end of it, all 24 champions lay dead, so battle was joined after all (vv.14–17).

Joab's men prevailed in a fierce engagement. Seeing the battle was lost, Abner made good his escape. However, he was spotted and chased by Asahel, one of Joab's brothers, who could run like the wind. He soon caught up with Abner, who strongly advised Asahel to go after one of the other soldiers, or risk being killed. Asahel refused to heed Abner's warnings, so Abner had no choice but to kill Asahel reluctantly in self-defence (vv.18–23).

Joab and Abishai, enraged by what had happened to their brother Asahel, pursued Abner. But by the time they caught up with him it was getting dark, and Abner had regrouped his forces. Abner proposed a cessation of hostilities, to which Joab agreed. Joab then re-assembled his troops, and marched back to Hebron through the night (vv.24–32). It seems that Joab never forgot what Abner had done. The fact that Abner had killed Asahel in self-defence cut no ice with Joab. Abner had killed his brother, and that was all there was to it. Joab was determined Abner wouldn't get away with it, and waited for an opportunity for revenge to occur.

A done deal

The longer the civil war went on, the more it became clear that David's forces would ultimately triumph. Abner was no fool, and saw the way the wind was blowing. He was also aware of the prophecies concerning David (3:18). So, he sent messengers to David offering a deal: 'Make an agreement with me, and I will help to bring all Israel over to you' (v.12). David agreed to do this, on condition that his wife, Michal, be restored to him (see Chapter 14).

Abner then persuaded the elders of Israel and the Benjamites,

the tribe from which Saul's family came, to invite David to be
their king. Having secured their agreement, Abner went back to
Hebron to tell David of his success, and David threw a feast in his
honour. Abner then left in peace to bring all the tribal elders to
make a 'compact' with David in Hebron (vv.13–21).

While the deal between David and Abner was being negotiated,
Joab and his men were carrying out a raid, and knew nothing of
these developments. Imagine Joab's reaction to finding out on his
return that, in his absence, David had done a deal with their chief
enemy and rival for the kingdom, Abner (vv.22–23). Joab must
have been both furious and fearful: furious, because David had
seen fit to go behind his back and strike a deal with the man who
had killed his brother Asahel; fearful, because he saw Abner, his
brother's killer, as a potential rival for his position as commander
of David's men. Throughout his life, Joab was determined that
nobody was going to become leader of David's armed forces in
his place, no matter what he had to do to make sure this didn't
happen. He enjoyed the power and kudos of his position too
much to have it taken away from him.

'What have you done?'

Joab, in typical style, boldly confronted David about the matter,
asking 'What have you done?' (v.24). Joab left his uncle in no doubt
that he didn't trust Abner one little bit, and that Abner must have
had an ulterior motive for coming to Hebron: namely, to suss out
David's military situation. And, to cap it all, David had been naive
enough to let Abner go off to carry out his devious plan!

David's reply obviously didn't satisfy Joab, because, unknown
to his uncle, Joab sent messengers after Abner to bring him back
to Hebron on some pretext or other (v.26). With this mixture of
fury, fear and revenge simmering inside him, Joab went out to
meet Abner. He took him aside on the pretext of having a private
conversation with him, and cold-bloodedly stabbed the off-guard
Abner to death (v.27). By this act of blood-revenge, Joab had
avenged his brother Asahel.

When the news about what Joab had done reached David, he in turn could well have asked his nephew, 'What have you done?' David roundly condemned Joab publicly, proclaiming that he had nothing to do with Joab's act, and calling for the full consequences of Joab's deed to be visited upon his nephew's family for ever (vv.28–29). David would have been very angry with Joab for murdering Abner, because Abner was central to delivering the smooth unification of the kingdom under David's rule. Abner held the north in his hands, and now David's own military leader had gone and killed him for his own personal reasons. Civil war could easily erupt again as a result.

Uneasy relationship

To try and prevent such a scenario occurring, David insisted that Joab and his men attend Abner's funeral with their clothes torn and wearing sackcloth, the traditional symbols of mourning. They were to walk in front of the bier on which Abner's body was placed, while David himself walked behind it. David made a great public display of his grief over Abner's death, weeping aloud and singing a lament for Abner. It had the desired effect, and renewed civil war was averted (vv.31–37).

In his post-funeral speech to his men, David made an extraordinary comment: 'though I am the anointed king, I am weak, and these sons of Zeruiah are too strong for me' (v.39). In these words is encapsulated the uneasy relationship David had with Joab during his reign. On the one hand, David knew that Joab had many desirable qualities. He was an excellent strategist and, perhaps most important of all, Joab was fiercely loyal to him. On the other hand, he knew that Joab was totally ruthless and cruel, and was always likely to do as he saw fit rather than submit to the wishes of the king. Because David realised how much he relied on Joab, he was prepared to 'cut him some slack' and overlook his shortcomings. Therefore, Joab remained unpunished for the murder of Abner.

Are we in any uneasy relationships at the moment? Are we

part of a group that is leading us away from God? Do we tolerate wrong behaviour from certain people because we are desperate to retain their friendship? Are we suffering because of blind loyalty to someone? Are we involved with a person who is not God-centred in their outlook? It can be very difficult to break off close relationships, but shouldn't we be asking ourselves whether this liaison is bringing us nearer to God, or taking us away from Him, and act accordingly (1 Cor. 5:9–11; 2 Cor. 6:14)?

The capture of Jerusalem

After David was anointed king over all Israel at Hebron, he marched on Jerusalem, also known as Zion. The city was so well fortified that it was easy to defend from attackers. The Jebusites, a Canaanite tribe who lived there, were so confident Jerusalem was impregnable that they taunted David with the words: 'You will not get in here; even the blind and the lame can ward you off' (5:6). But David was determined to conquer Jerusalem and make it his capital. The city was strategically well placed, being virtually at the centre of the newly united kingdom, as well as standing on a high ridge, making it visible for miles around.

The question was, how were they going to conquer it? Jerusalem's main water supply came from the Gihon spring outside the city walls, and was conducted within by means of a series of water shafts and tunnels. Joab volunteered to lead an attack on the city through this underground network, and took the Jebusites completely by surprise. The success of Joab's attack earned him the position of commander-in-chief of all the armies now under David's command as king of the whole of Israel (1 Chron. 11:6).

David called Jerusalem 'the City of David', and set about extending the area around the main fortress. Perhaps surprisingly it was Joab, who was famed for his exploits in war rather than his achievements in civil engineering, who 'restored the rest of the city' (1 Chron. 11:8). Then David brought the ark of God to Jerusalem amidst great celebrations and rejoicing (see Chapter 14).

The death of Uriah (2 Samuel 11)
The ruse

Some time later, David sent Joab and the entire Israelite army off to fight the Ammonites while he stayed behind in Jerusalem. Under Joab's leadership, the Israelites completely destroyed the Ammonites, and laid siege to their capital city of Rabbah (11:1).

A few months later, Joab received a strange communiqué from David. It simply read, 'Send me Uriah the Hittite' (v.6). Joab must have been surprised by such a request in the middle of a campaign, but his was not to reason why. When Joab sent for him, Uriah must have been amazed at being told that the king wanted to see him, but he dutifully set off for Jerusalem.

Joab had no inkling of what David had been up to, and how the king was about to go to great lengths to make sure Uriah slept with his wife, Bathsheba, during his stay in Jerusalem (vv.6–13). Neither Joab nor Uriah knew that Bathsheba was pregnant by David (vv.2–5), and that this was all a ruse cooked up by the king to cover up his adultery.

Plan B

David's efforts were all in vain, as the valiant Uriah refused to take advantage of the offer of home comforts. So David had to resort to Plan B. The next thing Joab knew, Uriah was back at the front bearing a letter from David, which effectively contained the Hittite's death warrant: 'Put Uriah in the front line where the fighting is fiercest. Then withdraw from him so that he will be struck down and die' (v.15).

There was a calculated cruel callousness about this plan of David's that Joab himself might have been proud of. He certainly didn't question the king's order; indeed, Joab seems to have implemented it almost immediately. 'So while Joab had the city under siege, he put Uriah at a place where he knew the strongest defenders were' (v.16) and the inevitable happened – Uriah was killed in battle (v.17).

Did Joab have no conscience at all? It's one thing to send

soldiers into battle, but to deliberately target one of them for death is surely something completely different. But then, what could Joab do about it? He would no doubt say that he was only obeying orders. As we know, that reasoning has been used countless times down the years to justify committing the most heinous crimes.

Do we ever override our conscience? What excuses do we use for doing things that we know are not right in God's sight? How do we justify our wrong actions? As David found out, to go against what God says is to start down a slippery slope that can only end in disaster, and not just for us, but for all those whom our wrong actions touch.

Joab's report

Joab sent a messenger to David to give him a full account of the battle at Rabbah. Joab had obviously implemented a somewhat reckless strategy, presumably to make sure Uriah got killed, because he told the messenger that the king might be angry at his report (vv.19–20). If he was angry, then the messenger was to say, 'Also, your servant Uriah the Hittite is dead' (v.21).

On hearing of the death of Uriah, David told the messenger to encourage Joab by saying: 'Don't let this upset you; the sword devours one as well as another. Press the attack against the city and destroy it' (v.25). Presumably this was code for 'Well done, mate! Don't worry; you're in the clear. That's the end of it.'

It may have been so as far as Joab was concerned, but David was in for a shock. Although he didn't know it when he sent that message to Joab, David was about to have a visit from Nathan the prophet, which would bring him to his knees in repentance. It would also bring him to write Psalm 51, a cry for God's mercy and forgiveness, which can be used by us all.

The trouble with Absalom (2 Samuel 13-20)
Reconciliation

Although David repented of his sin with Bathsheba, and experienced God's forgiveness, Nathan told him that the consequences of his sin would bring calamity upon his household (12:11–12). This prediction was partly fulfilled through the actions of Absalom. Like his father, Absalom was handsome and a natural leader. He may have been headstrong and hot-headed, but he was very popular with the people. When Absalom had his half-brother Amnon killed in revenge for raping his sister Tamar (13:28–29), he fled the country. David was devastated at what Absalom had done, and mourned for Amnon for three years.

Meanwhile, Joab was getting worried about the succession. For the good of both the nation and his own position, Joab wanted to make sure that there was a smooth transition of power after David's death. With Amnon, David's firstborn and heir, now dead, Absalom was next in line. It seems that Joab tried to persuade his uncle to restore Absalom to the court. When his efforts proved unsuccessful, Joab resorted to an elaborate charade (14:1–21).

Joab sent a 'wise woman' to David to spin him a yarn about her supposed family situation to get the king to agree that the welfare of the whole family was more important than a particular member being punished. When David did so, the woman said, 'When the king says this, does he not convict himself, for the king has not brought back his banished son?' (v.13). David then realised that Joab had put the woman up to this (v.19). He sent for Joab and said, 'Very well, I will do it. Go, bring back the young man Absalom' (v.21).

If Joab thought that everything was now settled, he was very much mistaken. Although Absalom was allowed to live in Jerusalem, David didn't bring him back to the court. After two years of this, Absalom's resentment boiled over. He sent for Joab to speak to David on his behalf. When Joab refused to come, Absalom set one of Joab's fields on fire to get his attention, which says a lot about Absalom (vv.28–30). Joab then told Absalom that he would speak to the king, who agreed to be reconciled to his son. But the seeds of rebellion against his father had been sown in Absalom's heart.

In my experience, being reconciled to someone is not easy, particularly if we have been wronged and deeply hurt by the actions of another person. But Jesus commands us to be reconciled with one another before we come to worship God (Matt. 5:23–24). This suggests that having something against another person is an obstacle to our worshipping God with integrity; that anger, resentment, bitterness and hatred are barriers not only between us and the person concerned, but also between us and God. Could that be why there are times in our lives when we don't feel close to God any more; times when our worship seems unfulfilling; times when our prayers just seem to bounce back off the ceiling?

Rebellion

Over the next few years, Absalom 'stole the hearts of the men of Israel' (15:6). In the end, David had to decide whether to stay in Jerusalem and face a siege, or make a run for it. Not wanting Jerusalem to be damaged, David chose the latter course, which also gave him time to marshal what remained of his forces to fight Absalom's army.

Although Joab had previously seen Absalom as David's successor, his arrogant decision to rebel against the king changed everything in Joab's eyes. Joab remained loyal to David, as did his brother, Abishai. Along with Ittai the Gittite, they were to lead David's troops into battle against Absalom's army. Absalom had appointed Amasa, a relative of Joab, as commander of his forces. As they went out to battle, David commanded Joab, Abishai and Ittai, in the hearing of the troops, 'Be gentle with the young man Absalom for my sake' (18:5).

The battle took place in and around the forest of Ephraim. Carnage resulted, but David's men were victorious. Although they were well outnumbered, Joab was more tactically astute, and his men knew the terrain much better than Absalom's forces. In the heat of the battle, Absalom came face to face with some of David's men in the forest. Absalom 'was riding his mule, and as the mule went under the thick branches of a large oak, Absalom's head got caught in the tree. He was left hanging in mid-air, while the mule he was riding kept on going' (v.9). What an amusing picture that paints! But it was no laughing matter for Absalom. The men left Absalom hanging there by his long hair, and rushed back to tell Joab.

When Joab berated them for not killing Absalom, they reminded Joab of what the king had said concerning his son. What happened next is another example of Joab's utter ruthlessness in doing what he thought was best in the situation, and taking matters into his own hands, rather than submitting to the wishes of the king. Being the pragmatist that he was, Joab would have realised that as long as Absalom remained alive, he would present a threat to the throne of David, even if the king couldn't see this himself.

Taking three javelins in his hand, Joab cold-bloodedly plunged them into Absalom's heart as he hung from the tree by his hair. And, if that wasn't enough, ten of Joab's armour-bearers then struck Absalom and killed him (vv.14–15). Joab blew a trumpet, stopping his troops from pursuing Absalom's army, and had Absalom's body thrown into a pit in the forest, and a large pile of rocks heaped on top.

Confrontation and humiliation

When he heard the news of Absalom's death, David went into deep decline, bemoaning the fate of his son. David's public display of weeping and mourning took the gloss off his army's spectacular victory (18:33–19:4). Joab was totally disgusted by the king's behaviour, and went to confront him about it in typical style. Joab certainly didn't mince his words: 'Today you have humiliated all your men, who have just saved your life ... You love those who hate you and hate those who love you. You have made it clear today that the commanders and their men mean nothing to you. I see that you would be pleased if Absalom were alive today and all of us were dead' (19:5–6). Joab's parting shot was that if David wanted an army left by the morning, he would go out right now and encourage his men, thanking them for what they had done.

David took Joab's advice, but never forgave him for killing Absalom. Shortly after this incident, David humiliated Joab by replacing him with Amasa, the commander of Absalom's army (v.13). David must have thought this move was a masterstroke, as it would unite the warring forces in the kingdom together, and punish Joab for his crimes at the same time. However, David should have known how Joab would react to this, given what had occurred years before when he made a deal with Abner.

Sure enough, when Joab met up with Amasa, he took the opportunity to catch him off guard and brutally stab him to death (20:8–10). Joab and Abishai than went on to deal decisively with a rebellion led by a man named Sheba, which Amasa had clearly failed to do. This action seems to have resulted in Joab being restored to his position (v.23).

The wrong side (1 Kings 1:5–2:34)
Adonijah

With Amnon and Absalom dead, Joab looked round for the best candidate to succeed the ageing king. Although David had pronounced that Solomon was to be his successor, Joab backed Adonijah. He must have felt very strongly about this, because his decision caused him to break his lifetime loyalty to David. Joab was supported in this by no less a personage than Abiathar, the high priest.

Adonijah was actually the next in line to the throne, and considered his father's pronouncement to be unimportant. After all, if the commander-in-chief of the army and the high priest were both on his side, who could stand against him? So, buoyed up by such support, he went ahead and held a feast to proclaim himself king (1:5,7,9–10). But for once in his life, Joab had backed the wrong side.

Having been made aware of what was afoot, David declared that Solomon be anointed and proclaimed king forthwith. Adonijah and his supporters were still feasting when they heard the sound of the trumpet and the people shouting 'Long live King Solomon!' (v.39). When they found out what had occurred, Adonijah and Joab ran to the court of the tabernacle and took hold of the horns of the altar, thus seeking refuge under God's protection (v.50; 2:28).

No mercy

Solomon granted Adonijah a reprieve, but not Joab. Reminding Solomon of how Joab had killed both Abner and Amasa in peacetime, 'and with that blood stained the belt round his waist and the sandals on his feet', David had counselled Solomon to 'Deal with him according to your wisdom, but do not let his grey head go down to the grave in peace' (2:5–6).

Joab's murderous actions obviously carried more weight in David's mind than all the years of faithful and loyal service that Joab had given him. Joab never lost a battle, and was key to establishing David's kingdom. But both David and Solomon knew that Joab was a dangerous man to have around. Besides which, it was important that the house of David was seen to be guiltless of Joab's crimes, and that Joab was seen to be executed by the king at last for what he had done.

Solomon sent Benaiah to carry out the execution of Joab. Although Benaiah seemed reluctant to kill Joab there in the tabernacle, Solomon had no compunction about ordering him to do exactly that, on the grounds that this act was divine retribution for Joab's evil acts, and would bring lasting peace to the house and descendants of David (vv.31–33).

And so it was that Joab came to an ignominious end there in the tabernacle, killed by Benaiah while desperately clutching the horns of the altar. He who had shown no mercy received no mercy. Benaiah replaced Joab as commander-in-chief, while Zadok became high priest in place of Abiathar, marking the end of Eli's priestly line (see Chapter 13).

Joab lived his life by his own standards rather than by God's, and this ultimately led to his downfall. Are we seeking to live our lives by God's standards, or by our own? As Solomon himself would write years later, maybe with Joab in mind, 'There is a way that seems right to a man, but in the end it leads to death' (Prov. 14:12). May we all heed the warning, and live our lives God's way, which will ultimately lead to eternal life.

Chapter 16

Lacking Wisdom

Rehoboam

2 Chronicles 10–12

(Other bit part players appearing: Adoniram, Shemaiah, Shishak)

Subject to negotiation

King Solomon appointed his son, Rehoboam, as his successor, even though he was not his firstborn. Rehoboam was forty-one years old when he became king of Israel. His mother, Naamah, was an Ammonite, one of the many foreign princesses Solomon had married in order to secure political alliances with the surrounding nations and consolidate his kingdom. Rehoboam would have been brought up in the lap of luxury, and enjoyed the privileged upbringing befitting a future king. However, he must have been aware that there was unrest among the northern tribes of the kingdom.

Rehoboam would also have known about his father's dealings with a man named Jeroboam. Ahijah the prophet had told Jeroboam that he would one day become king of the ten northern tribes. Solomon tried to kill Jeroboam, but he managed to escape to Egypt, and was living there under the protection of Shishak, the Pharaoh (see Chapter 17).

Following the procedure which happened when his grandfather David became king (2 Sam. 2:4; 5:3), it seems that Rehoboam had to be proclaimed king over the tribes of Judah and Benjamin in the south, and then separately as king over the ten northern tribes, thus confirming his position as ruler of the whole of Israel. It also appears that this act of allegiance by the northern tribes was subject to negotiation. So Rehoboam went to the city of Shechem, which lay about thirty miles to the north of Jerusalem, to meet the representatives of the northern tribes on their ground (10:1).

Conflicting advice

When he arrived in Shechem, Rehoboam must have been perturbed to discover that Jeroboam had returned from Egypt, and had been asked by the northern tribal leaders to head up their negotiations (vv.2–3). Rehoboam must have felt somewhat put out at having to negotiate with this man, whom he would have looked down on as an upstart and a rebel. It probably came as a surprise to Rehoboam, therefore, that Jeroboam and his fellow-leaders were prepared to acknowledge him as king – albeit on one condition: that he would lighten the forced labour requirements and excessive tax load that his father Solomon had placed upon them in order to fulfil his building programme (v.4).

At least Rehoboam didn't dismiss their request out of hand, but asked for three days in which to consider their proposition. First of all, he sought the opinion of his father's counsellors. They advised Rehoboam to show kindness and consideration towards these people, because that approach would result in them happily serving him as their king (vv.6–7). Then Rehoboam turned to his contemporaries for their opinion. They advised him to do the complete opposite, and to tell the northern tribes that, if they thought times were tough under his father Solomon, then they 'ain't seen nothing yet!' (vv.9–11). They suggested Rehoboam used the well-known proverb 'My little finger is thicker than my father's waist' (v.10) in his response, meaning that Rehoboam's weakest impositions would be much stronger than the strongest measures carried out by his father.

Rehoboam made the unwise and fateful decision to take the advice of his mates rather than listen to the wisdom of his father's generation (v.8). In a situation which required tact and sensitivity, Rehoboam opted for the hard, arrogant approach. Clearly, he believed that to make concessions would be taken as a sign of weakness, and that people could be bullied into obedience and loyalty. His strong-arm tactics were to rebound on him with a vengeance.

To whom do we turn for advice? Do we go to those we know will tell us what we want to hear, or to those who will be honest and straight with us? Do we only ever consult our contemporaries, or are we wise enough to listen to the opinion of our elders? It certainly helps to talk things through with someone who has our best interests at heart, and that includes God. We are told that 'If any of you lacks wisdom, he should ask God, who gives generously … without finding fault, and it will be given to him' (James 1:5).

This had been a wonderful opportunity for Rehoboam to be gracious and statesmanlike, and win the respect and loyalty of this troublesome group of leaders. But he blew it completely, and consequently he blew his kingdom apart. No longer was there any hope of maintaining any semblance of unity in this kingdom, which was in fact nothing more than a loose confederation of tribes. Rehoboam showed a complete lack of wisdom by choosing to be confrontational and not to listen. All this did was to antagonise 80 per cent of his subjects, and set Israel on a course from which it would never recover.

The kingdom divides

On hearing of Rehoboam's intentions, and angered by the fact that the king wasn't prepared to listen to their grievances,

Jeroboam and the northern tribal representatives stormed out in high dudgeon, to the same rallying cry used in an unsuccessful, short-lived rebellion against King David (2 Sam. 20:1). Except this rebellion would be successful and long-lasting.

Rehoboam sent Adoniram after them to try and retrieve the situation. Adoniram was not really a wise choice to put it mildly, because he was the minister 'in charge of forced labour' (v.18)! This must have been like a red rag to a bull as far as Jeroboam and his cronies were concerned. Not surprisingly, 'the Israelites stoned him to death' (v.18), but Rehoboam managed to escape back to Jerusalem.

News that Jeroboam had returned from Egypt spread across the northern territories. An assembly was convened, at which Jeroboam was crowned king of the ten northern tribes of Israel (1 Kings 12:20). Only the tribes of Judah and Benjamin remained loyal to Rehoboam. On hearing of the secession of the ten tribes and the coronation of Jeroboam, Rehoboam mustered a vast army to bring the rebels to heel and reunite the kingdom. But God intervened through the prophet Shemaiah to prevent him doing this, saying, 'Do not go up to fight against your brothers ... for this is my doing' (11:4). To his credit, Rehoboam obeyed the word of the Lord and returned home.

Why would God do this? Why would he cause the kingdom of Israel to be split in two? Clearly, there was the punishment aspect to it. But could it have been because, if God had allowed Rehoboam to fight the northern tribes, he would have been defeated? Then Jeroboam would have become king, and David's line would have been broken in contravention of God's promise to David (2 Sam. 7:15–16). This way, David's line would be preserved, and God's plan for the Messiah to be descended from David would remain on course.

The prophecy of Ahijah had come to pass. The kingdom was now divided into two, and was generally seen as a split between David's tribe of Judah, supported by the small tribe of Benjamin, and the rest. The southern part therefore became known as

'Judah', from which the word 'Jew' is derived, with the majority in the northern part retaining the name 'Israel'. Throughout Rehoboam's reign, there were constant skirmishes between the armies of the two rival kingdoms (12:15).

Strengthened

Fearing he might find himself in a pincer movement between Israel in the north, and Jeroboam's apparent friend Egypt in the south, Rehoboam embarked on a programme of fortification (11:5–12). The defences of fifteen towns and cities were strengthened; each was given its own commander, along with emergency provisions and weapons. Thus Rehoboam strengthened not only his kingdom, but also his own position as king of Judah.

But there was another way in which the kingdom of Judah was strengthened at this time. Many God-fearing Israelites in the north, including priests and Levites, were horrified at the religious practices Jeroboam was instituting. He was even setting up his own priesthood, which encouraged idol worship (see Chapter 17). So they left Israel and flooded into Judah, thus giving the southern kingdom a spiritual impetus, and strengthening its religious life.

For three years, Rehoboam and his people followed the Lord, and prospered from their obedience to God (vv.13–17). Rehoboam's family flourished, and he appointed Abijah, the eldest son of his favourite wife Maacah, the daughter of Absalom, as his successor (v.22). During this period, Rehoboam is said to have 'acted wisely' (v.23). But, unfortunately, this state of affairs was not going to last.

Invasion

Interestingly, it was once Rehoboam felt established and secure as king that he and the people of Judah 'abandoned the law of the LORD' (12:1). Altars were built to foreign gods, poles were erected in honour of the Canaanite mother-goddess Asherah, shrine prostitutes were in evidence, and the people once more engaged in 'detestable practices' (1 Kings 14:24). Once again, Rehoboam had shown a lack of wisdom which would have far-reaching consequences.

It seems incredible that Rehoboam and his subjects would change their behaviour so dramatically, when following the Lord had brought peace, prosperity and stability to the kingdom of Judah. Could it be that they had become totally self-sufficient, and therefore felt they didn't need God any more? And isn't it often true that, when we are experiencing difficult times, we call upon the Lord, and place our faith and trust in Him – only to become more lax in our discipleship once the stormy times have passed, and we feel in control of our lives once again?

This state of affairs went on for two years, until in the fifth year of Rehoboam's reign, Shishak, king of Egypt, invaded Judah. This was God's punishment on the sinfulness and unfaithfulness of the people (v.2). Rehoboam had come to trust in his fortified cities for protection rather than in the Lord. He was surely shaken as these cities, which must have been his pride and joy, fell one by one to the massive invading armies from the south. Now Jerusalem itself was threatened (vv.3–4).

Right reaction

Rehoboam and his elders gathered in the capital, quaking with fear. They only seem to have made the connection between their idolatry and the Egyptian invasion after Shemaiah the prophet came to see them, and pointed it out (v.5). The reaction of Rehoboam and the leaders of Judah was admirable – they 'humbled themselves and said, "The LORD is just"' (v.6).

In my experience, that is not a reaction it's always easy to emulate! But if we are prepared to humble ourselves, both individually and as God's people, we know that God's blessing will be poured out upon us (2 Chron. 7:14; Luke 14:11). Because Rehoboam and the elders reacted in the right way, and accepted the wisdom of the Lord's judgment, God decided that they would not perish at the hand of the Egyptian invader.

Although Shishak ransacked Jerusalem and plundered the Temple, carrying off all 'the treasures of the temple of the LORD and the treasures of the royal palace' (v.9), Rehoboam and his entourage were spared. According to Egyptian records, Shishak's troops went as far north as the Sea of Galilee – well into the northern kingdom. Eventually, however, Shishak realised he had overreached himself, and gradually withdrew back to Egypt, taking all his plunder with him.

Keeping up appearances

Included in the booty taken from the Temple were 'the gold shields that Solomon had made' (v.9) – all 500 of them (1 Kings 10:16–17). Rehoboam's reaction to this is fascinating. He decided that the shields were to be replaced. It was important to keep up appearances, even though the 'golden age' of his father and grandfather had gone for good. The impoverished kingdom could no longer afford gold; so bronze was used instead as a cheap imitation of the real thing. How diminished Solomon's kingdom had become! So, 'Whenever the king went to the LORD's temple, the guards went with him, bearing the shields, and afterwards they returned them to the guardroom' (v.11).

Did Rehoboam lock the shields away so that the people couldn't get a close look at them and see that they were not gold at all, but bronze? Did Rehoboam go through this charade in an attempt to pretend that nothing had changed: that everything was just the same as before the invasion? Did he maintain this elaborate pretence to avoid being humiliated in the eyes of the people? Whatever the reason, this hypocrisy was maintained to mask the reality.

Do we ever go to church just to keep up appearances when, in reality, our heart is far from God? Do we put on a show, even though there is no substance to it any more? Do we pretend that nothing has happened or changed, when deep down we know that it has? If we are honest, we all do this at times. And we can fool most of the people most of the time, but never God. Yet, although God knows the reality of our situation, He never condemns us, but in His mercy waits to restore us, and turn the bronze of our spiritual poverty back into the gold of the spiritual wealth that comes from a close relationship with Him.

Rehoboam sought to worship God on the cheap. The bronze cost him next to nothing compared with what the gold would have cost him.

In our daily lives, do we bring God worship which, like bronze, costs us little? Or do we, like King David, seek to bring Him worship which, like gold, costs us much (1 Chron. 21:24)?

The final verdict

It seems that Rehoboam did return to the Lord after these events, for a while at least, because it is recorded that 'there was some good in Judah' (v.12). But, sadly, he continually wavered in his commitment to God. So the overall verdict on Rehoboam's seventeen-year reign was that 'He did evil because he had not set his heart on seeking the LORD' (v.14). Rehoboam patently lacked his father's wisdom, and was responsible for the nation irrevocably being torn in two, ultimately with disastrous consequences for both the kingdoms of Judah and Israel.

What an opportunity Rehoboam wasted to build on the inheritance he received from his grandfather, David, and his father, Solomon! He inherited a powerful, wealthy kingdom. Five years later, it had crumbled away. The challenge for us is surely this: Are we building on the Christian heritage we have received from our forebears, or are we just maintaining appearances, when the truth is that it is crumbling away? God is looking for a people who, unlike Rehoboam, have hearts that are set on seeking Him and His ways unwaveringly in these increasingly difficult days.

Chapter 17

Downhill to Destruction

Jeroboam

1 Kings 11:26–14:20
(Other bit part players appearing: Ahijah, Abijah)

Promotion and prophecy

Jeroboam, the son of Nebat, came from the tribe of Ephraim, one of the northern tribes of Israel. His mother was a widow named Zeruah, and his family were of humble origins (11:26). Jeroboam was brought to the attention of King Solomon for his excellent work during the rebuilding projects in Jerusalem. Not only was he a good worker, but Jeroboam was also popular among the men. So Solomon made him the foreman of the entire workforce drawn from the northern tribes (vv.27–28). This workforce was engaged in the Millo project: the rebuilding of the terraces and part of the city wall. As foreman, he would have become the focal point for all the expressions of disgruntled resentment from the men, both as workers and taxpayers, as their exploitation by King Solomon grew progressively worse.

Shortly after this promotion, something very unusual happened to Jeroboam. He was on his way out of Jerusalem one day, when he encountered a prophet of God named Ahijah, who came from the shrine at Shiloh (see Chapter 13). There were just the two of them there on the road. Interestingly, both Ahijah and Jeroboam were Ephraimites, the strongest of the northern tribes.

Ahijah then did something which would have had Jeroboam gasping in amazement, and wondering if his eyes were deceiving him. The prophet stopped, took off his cloak, which was obviously brand new, and proceeded to rip it up into twelve pieces. Ahijah then told Jeroboam to take ten of the twelve pieces and keep them for himself (vv.29–31).

Jeroboam's mouth must have been wide open in astonishment by now, and probably stayed that way as Ahijah went on to explain what his dramatic actions were all about. Ahijah told Jeroboam that God was going to 'tear the kingdom out of Solomon's hand and give you ten tribes' (v.31). The kingdom was going to be taken from Solomon's successor and split in two as punishment for the nation's worship of foreign gods. David and Solomon's descendants would rule over their own tribe of Judah, which would be supported by only one other tribe: Benjamin (see Chapter 16). The other ten northern tribes would be given to Jeroboam to rule over (vv.32–36).

Always there

We can only imagine how Jeroboam must have felt as Ahijah pronounced God's plan and will for him with these words: 'However, as for you, I will take you, and you will rule over all that your heart desires; you will be king over Israel. If you do whatever I command you and walk in my ways and do what is right in my eyes by keeping my statutes and commands, as David my servant did, I will be with you. I will build you a dynasty as enduring as the one I built for David and will give Israel to you' (vv.37–38). Some prophecy! Ironically, it is reminiscent of the prophecy given to Solomon (1 Kings 9:4–5). Solomon had failed in the areas that really mattered to God. Would Jeroboam do any better?

Although most of us are never going to rule a kingdom, God's wonderful promise 'I will be with you' is just as much for us as it was for Jeroboam. God has promised to be always there with us, whatever trials and tribulations we may have to go through in our lives. God's Word declares: 'When you pass through the waters, I will be with you ... When you walk through the fire, you will not be burned'; 'Never will I leave you; never will I forsake you' (Isa. 43:2; Heb. 13:5).

Having experienced God being with me in some testing times recently, I felt moved to write a song entitled *Always There* to encourage us not to be afraid in such situations, and to put our faith and trust in God. The song includes these words:

> In the midst of your trials, I will be with you;
> When dark times come upon you, do not despair.
> For I am your deliverer, your rock, your shield, your refuge;
> So do not be afraid, for I am always there.
>
> Faithful God, always there with me,
> Faithful God, beside me constantly;
> O what a faithful God you are;
> Always there, always there, always there with me.

Return from exile

What Jeroboam did next is unclear. It is recorded that he 'rebelled against the king' (v.26), but what form that rebellion took is not mentioned. Whether as a punishment for that, or because the king had got to hear about Ahijah's prophecy, or maybe for both reasons, Solomon tried to kill Jeroboam. However, Jeroboam managed to escape the king's clutches, and fled down south to Egypt, where he received the protection of the Pharaoh, Shishak (v.40).

After the death of Solomon, Jeroboam returned from exile (see Chapter 16). The elders of the northern tribes welcomed him back as their leader, and asked him to head up their accession negotiations with the new king, Rehoboam, whom Jeroboam probably regarded as a spoilt brat. Jeroboam must have been delighted that the elders had not forgotten him. Interestingly, he doesn't seem to have tried to force Ahijah's prophecy to come to pass. Presumably he didn't tell the leaders about it when he met up with them in Shechem to carry out the negotiations, but rather went along with their conditional intention of accepting Rehoboam as king. Perhaps Jeroboam had the faith to believe that God would bring about what He had promised in His way and in His time, and was prepared to wait.

In my experience, such patience is often rare among us. When God promises us something, are we not inclined to expect to see it sooner rather than later, and even take steps to 'encourage' it to happen? How often does God need to remind us that 'my thoughts are not your thoughts, neither are your ways my ways' (Isa. 55:8)? Isn't it always better to wait for God's moment, because that's always perfectly timed?

Rebellion

In the event, Rehoboam made it crystal clear that he was not going to listen to their demands or accommodate their conditions (12:12–15). Perhaps Jeroboam knew this was inevitable, and would force a showdown. Rehoboam's arrogant attitude, and his stated intention of making things much worse for the northern tribes, must have annoyed them intensely. Jeroboam and all the elders stormed out, with rebellious words on their lips which declared their intent to revolt (v.16). Was it then that Jeroboam told the elders about Ahijah's prophecy?

Rehoboam's gaffe in sending Adoniram, of all people, to try and humour the northern elders backfired spectacularly. Adoniram was the man in charge of the forced labour they were all complaining about! His arrival just made the situation worse. Jeroboam and the elders saw it as a total insult, and stoned the hapless Adoniram to death (v.18). The elders then decided unanimously to form their own kingdom, and all the people of the northern tribes gathered together to crown the charismatic Jeroboam as their king (v.20). The prophecy of Ahijah had been fulfilled. The nation was divided into two kingdoms: Judah in the south and Israel in the north (see Chapter 16).

Convenient worship

Although full-scale civil war had been averted, the two armies frequently clashed over the years. Like Rehoboam in the south, Jeroboam felt the need to secure his kingdom, so he fortified the cities of Shechem and Peniel (v.25). Surprisingly, in view of the acclaim he had received, Jeroboam seems to have felt insecure as king of Israel. His fear was that, if the men in his kingdom continued to go to the Temple in Jerusalem, Rehoboam's capital, for the three annual festivals, as they were required to do (Deut. 16:16), sooner or later they would kill him and transfer their allegiance back to Rehoboam. Even though God had promised Jeroboam that his future was secure and his dynasty would be lasting (v.38), he decided to take matters into his own hands. Like many of us, he just couldn't bring himself to simply trust in God and not worry about the situation (Matt. 6:25–34).

Jeroboam's solution to the problem he thought he had was both dramatic and traumatic, and was driven by his unfounded fear. He set up shrines where the people could come to worship, instead of having to trail all the way down south to Jerusalem. One shrine was at Bethel, in the south of Israel, about twelve miles to the north of Jerusalem; the other was at Dan, in the most northerly area of his kingdom (vv.28–29). Jeroboam set up these centres of worship specifically to rival the Temple in Jerusalem.

The choice of Bethel as the location for one of these shrines was ironic, because in the past it had been a place that symbolised commitment to God. For example, it was the place where Jacob had recommitted his life to God (Gen. 28:16–22). As a result of Jeroboam's actions, Bethel would now become a byword for wickedness and idolatry, and in the future attract the scathing criticism of the prophets Hosea and Amos for its sinfulness and godlessness (Hosea 4:15–17; 10:8; Amos 5:4–6).

The idea of worshipping at one of these centres was an attractive proposition for the men of the north, as it was much more convenient. But it meant that they were disobeying God by so doing. Jeroboam must have known this as well as anyone, yet he actively encouraged his subjects to be disobedient and worship there, saying, 'It is too much for you to go up to Jerusalem' (v.28).

And there's more!

But that wasn't all. 'After seeking advice' (v.28), presumably from the tribal elders, Jeroboam decided to erect a golden calf at both shrines (v.29). In those days in that part of the world, pagan deities were often portrayed standing on calves or bulls, which were common symbols of strength and fertility. Jeroboam made the same mistake Aaron had made back in the wilderness years; they both tried to combine the pagan symbol of the calf with the worship of God, although neither of them attempted to actually fashion a statue of Jehovah God standing on the calf.

Jeroboam's proclamation to the people, 'Here are your gods, O Israel, who brought you up out of Egypt' (v.28), is virtually identical to the words spoken by Aaron (Exod. 32:4). With the people of the north now worshipping the golden calves at Jeroboam's shrines, history was repeating itself. They were sinning against God by breaking the second commandment again (v.30).

Jeroboam further compounded this sin by building smaller shrines on various 'high places', and appointing priests 'from all sorts of people, even though they were not Levites' (v.31). This was in direct disobedience of God's command (Num. 3:5–10), and resulted in many legitimate priests, Levites, and God-fearing Israelites streaming out of Israel and setting up home in Judah (see Chapter 16). Jeroboam even instituted his own version of the Feast of Tabernacles to replace this annual, national festival (vv.32–33).

In fact, what Jeroboam had done was to set up nothing less than a completely new religious system and structure in the north, whether he originally intended to do so or not. As a result, the floodgates were now open for the kingdom of Israel to become completely contaminated by worship of the pagan deities of their neighbours, such as Baal. The division into two kingdoms was no longer just physical – it was now spiritual as well.

Whose way?

By his actions, Jeroboam had angered God in five ways: building alternative shrines to the Temple in Jerusalem; setting up the golden calves, and proclaiming them as gods to be worshipped; building more shrines on the high places and encouraging the people to worship there; appointing priests who were not from the tribe of Levi and were corrupt; instituting his own festival.

Jeroboam had decided to do things his way, not God's. These acts would have disastrous consequences for both Jeroboam, whose family was eventually destroyed, and the kingdom of Israel. Jeroboam had set a pattern which his successors would follow, and in so doing would earn this typical kind of condemnation: 'He walked in all the ways of Jeroboam son of Nebat and in his sin, which he had caused Israel to commit, so that they provoked the LORD, the God of Israel, to anger by their worthless idols' (1 Kings 16:26).

Are we doing things our way, or God's way? Are our lives submitted to God's will, or does our will prevail? When we are afraid, or feeling insecure and under pressure, as Jeroboam was, we can soon find ourselves taking matters into our own hands in a desperate attempt to resolve the situation, or to escape from it.

In my experience, this usually results in things going from bad to worse, as it did for Jeroboam. Isn't it better to commit our way to God, and do things His way? As Solomon himself wrote: 'Trust in the LORD with all your heart and lean not on your own understanding; in all your ways acknowledge him, and he will make your paths straight' (Prov. 3:5–6). Jeroboam chose to ignore such sound advice, and suffered the consequences.

The prophet of God

It wasn't long before God's anger in the face of what Jeroboam had done became known. A prophet from Judah arrived in Bethel with a message from God (13:1–3). The fact that he came from Judah would seem to indicate God's rejection of the religious, though not political, division that Jeroboam had brought about. The prophet launched into a tirade against what was now happening in Bethel, prophesying that the pagan priests would be sacrificed on their own altars during the reign of a future king named Josiah (see Chapter 25).

Jeroboam was furious at what the prophet had said against Bethel. He stretched out his arm, presumably to point an accusing finger at the prophet, and commanded that the man of God be seized. As he did so, there were two dramatic occurrences. The hand that Jeroboam had stretched out towards the prophet 'shrivelled up, so that he could not pull it back' (v.4); and, almost simultaneously, 'the altar ... split apart and its ashes poured out' (v.5) as a confirmation that what the prophet had said was true, and would come to pass. It did so in every respect 300 years later (2 Kings 23:1–20).

Opportunity

As a result of these dramatic happenings, Jeroboam's attitude to the prophet changed completely, although it seems this was due entirely to self-interest rather than to repentance for what he had done. He had the temerity to ask the prophet to 'Intercede with the LORD your God and pray for me that my hand may be restored' (v.6). To his great credit, the prophet was prepared to do this, in spite of the way Jeroboam had treated him. Do we pray for people who treat us badly? In my experience, this is difficult to do, but it is what Jesus expects of us (Luke 6:27–28).

Here we see the great mercy of God. In spite of Jeroboam's sinfulness, God graciously healed him in response to the prayers of the prophet. Jeroboam responded to this act of mercy and grace by offering the prophet hospitality and a gift (v.7). He turned both of them down, explaining that he was acting in obedience to God (vv.8–10), a reminder to Jeroboam of his own disobedience to God by taking the measures he had in an attempt to secure his kingdom, instead of trusting God to fulfil His promise.

This was a God-given opportunity for Jeroboam to respond to God's mercy and grace, to repent of his wrong deeds, to restore his relationship with God, and to follow God's ways rather than his own. Sadly, he didn't take it, and just carried on as before – with disastrous consequences: 'Even after this, Jeroboam did not change his evil ways, but once more appointed priests for the high places from all sorts of people ... This was the sin of the house of Jeroboam that led to its downfall ...' (vv.33–34). This was inevitable, given that God's blessing on Jeroboam was conditional on him walking in God's ways and doing what was right in God's sight, as Jeroboam well knew from Ahijah's prophecy (11:38).

Tragedy

Some time later, one of Jeroboam's sons, Abijah, became ill. Knowing that Ahijah was still alive and living in Shiloh, Jeroboam sent his wife in disguise to consult the old prophet as to Abijah's fate. The irony was that the disguise was unnecessary because Ahijah was now blind, and Ahijah saw through it anyway! As Jeroboam's wife was on her way, God told Ahijah she was coming. So when she arrived, Ahijah called out, 'Come in, wife of Jeroboam'

(14:6), which must have been a bit of a shock for her.

Ahijah's tragic final prophecy concerning Jeroboam stands in direct and stark contrast to his first one. He launched into a tirade about all the evils of Jeroboam's reign and its dire consequences, not only for Jeroboam's family, but for the entire nation of Israel, which God would 'uproot' and 'scatter' (v.15). Ahijah certainly didn't spare her blushes, using very strong language and vivid imagery, such as 'I will burn up the house of Jeroboam as one burns dung, until it is all gone' (v.10). And he wasn't particularly sensitive when it came to telling her about the tragic fate of her son: 'When you set foot in your city, the boy will die' (v.12). Ahijah went on to say that God would raise up a king who would 'cut off the family of Jeroboam' (v.14). That king was Baasha (15:27–30). Ahijah told poor Jeroboam's wife that she was to relay all this information to her husband; not a task she must have been relishing as she journeyed home.

Shortly after this incident, Israel was at war with Judah (2 Chron. 13:2–20). Abijah was now king of Judah, having succeeded his father, Rehoboam. Ironically, he had the same name as the son of Jeroboam who had died. Abijah had 4,000 fighting men at his disposal, but was outnumbered two-to-one by Jeroboam's forces. Nevertheless, Abijah invaded Israel's territory, and the battle lines were drawn up. Interestingly, Jeroboam had taken the two golden calves to the battlefront, a mark of the depravity to which he had sunk. He was presumably relying on them to give him the victory. Jeroboam's reliance on idols signalled his doom. Although tactically and numerically Jeroboam had the advantage, Judah placed their faith and trust in God, not in idols. Jeroboam's forces were routed, and shortly afterwards, 'the LORD struck him down and he died' (2 Chron. 13:20).

Jeroboam was king of Israel for twenty-two years, and was succeeded by his son, Nadab. The tragedy of Jeroboam was that he had all the qualities to become a great king but, like Solomon before him, he failed in the areas of his life that really mattered to God. He allowed himself to be undermined by fear and, rather than consulting the Lord, he decided to do things his own way. What a marvellous opportunity Jeroboam was given by God to serve Him. But he failed to do so. What is it that stops us from serving God and taking the opportunities He gives us?

Chapter 18

A Reign of Two Parts

Asa

2 Chronicles 14–16
(Other bit part players appearing: Azariah, Baasha, Hanani)

The obedience effect

Asa succeeded his father, Abijah, as king of Judah, and reigned for forty-one years (16:13). Both his father and his grandfather, Rehoboam, were disobedient to God, and allowed idolatry to flourish in Judah. During their reigns, 'Judah did evil in the eyes of the LORD' (1 Kings 14:22; 15:3), although there were times when both Rehoboam and Abijah turned back to God, and prospered because of it (see Chapters 16–17). Indeed, this was a characteristic of the kings of Judah who succeeded them: they mainly did evil in God's sight, but some good was to be found in many of them. However, there were some who honoured and served God throughout the whole of their reigns, and restored the worship of the one true God in Judah.

Perhaps surprisingly in view of the largely bad example set by

Abijah and Rehoboam, Asa 'did what was good and right in the eyes of the LORD' (14:2). Maybe he had seen the advantages for the nation that were evident during those times when his father and grandfather did actually 'seek the Lord', and realised that pleasing God was the best thing to do all round. So Asa destroyed all the altars and shrines on the high places dedicated to the worship of false gods, smashing the sacred stones and cutting down the poles erected in honour of the Canaanite goddess Asherah. He turned the nation of Judah back to worship of the one true God, instructing them to obey God's laws and commands (vv.3–5).

The result of Asa's actions was that there were ten years of peace and economic prosperity in Judah. By contrast, during the time Asa was king of Judah, Israel was ruled by eight evil kings, and was in constant turmoil. During those years of peace, Asa prepared the nation against future troubles by building defences and strengthening their position (vv.6–7).

Obedience to God brought peace to Judah. In my experience, the same applies spiritually speaking. When we obey God, we are at peace with God. The Bible teaches us that God places a high value on obedience (1 Sam. 15:22). Jesus Himself was the greatest example of obedience: 'he humbled himself and became obedient to death – even death on a cross' (Phil. 2:8). If we are not at peace with God at the moment, could it be that we are being disobedient to Him by not following His commands in certain areas of our lives? If that is so, then should we not follow Asa's courageous example, and deal drastically with what is displeasing to God, that our peace with Him might be restored?

Faith in God

Having built up and equipped his army during those years of peace, Asa must have felt militarily secure – until Zerah the Cushite hove into view, that is! Zerah was probably the general of the Egyptian and Cushite forces, which vastly outnumbered the army of Judah. Humanly speaking, Asa would have known that they had no chance against this powerful array of military might assembled against them. Nevertheless, he led his army out to meet the Egyptians, and took up position ready for battle.

What tremendous faith in God Asa must have had to do this in the face of such overwhelming odds! He clearly believed with all his heart that God would give them the victory against this vastly superior force. Whether his troops were quite so sure is another matter. Having shown his faith by lining up his army for battle, Asa then spoke out his faith in the words of this amazing prayer: 'LORD, there is no-one like you to help the powerless against the mighty. Help us, O LORD our God, for we rely on you, and in your name we have come against this vast army. O LORD, you are our God; do not let man prevail against you' (v.11). The result was that, as the men of Judah engaged in battle with the invaders, God intervened, and brought about a great victory: 'The LORD struck down the Cushites ... they were crushed before the LORD and his forces' (14:12–13).

In my experience, there are times when we all feel powerless in the face of certain situations or overwhelmed by what comes against us. It really does feel like we are in a battle. When this happens, why not use Asa's prayer as a model? So we begin by acknowledging that there is no one like God, and reminding ourselves that, although we might feel powerless, He is all-powerful and can do anything. Then we admit our need, ask for God's help while expressing our faith and trust in God, and claim the victory in His name.

Interestingly, Asa prepared for battle before he prayed, and having prayed, he got stuck in. The Bible tells us that 'faith by itself, if it is not accompanied by action, is dead' (James 2:17). Let's be prepared to back up our expressions of faith by actions that show we really do believe and trust in God to answer our prayer, as Asa did.

Warning and encouragement

While Asa and his men were still relishing their victory, God sent Azariah to them with an important warning (15:1–6). They were to continue to stay close to God, to seek Him, and to remain steadfast in their commitment to Him. Azariah used the state of turmoil in Israel as an example of what would happen in Judah if they turned away from God. But his word of warning was balanced by a word of encouragement – 'be strong and do not give up, for your work will be rewarded' (v.7).

It seems to me that this warning and these words of encouragement are just as important for us to heed today. Are we staying close to God, seeking Him and His ways, and being totally committed to Him? Perhaps we are becoming complacent, as Judah was in danger of doing, congratulating ourselves on the steadfastness of our stand for God, and thinking nothing could ever happen to destroy that. That's why Paul warns us, 'if you think you are standing firm, be careful that you don't fall!' (1 Cor. 10:12).

But let's also be encouraged to persevere in our work for God's kingdom, in the knowledge that God sees all that we do, even if others don't. 'Let us not become weary in doing good' (Gal. 6:9), but continue to serve the Lord in such a way that one day He will be able to say to us, 'Well done, good and faithful servant!' (Matt. 25:21,23).

Radical steps

When Asa heard Azariah's prophecy, he was encouraged to take even more radical steps to firmly establish the worship of God in Judah. Asa realised that, although he had made a good start, he hadn't done nearly enough yet. So he went through his kingdom with a fine-tooth comb, destroying all vestiges of pagan worship; and then he did the same in the part of Ephraim that he had captured. He also 'repaired the altar of the LORD that was in front of the portico of the LORD's temple' (v.8).

Asa assembled the people of the kingdom of Judah together, and that included the large numbers of people who had come from the northern tribes of Ephraim, Manasseh and Simeon to settle in the land. These immigrants had 'come over to him from Israel when they saw that the LORD his God was with him' (v.9). Do people from outside the kingdom of God want to come and join our churches, because they can see that God is with us? Are they attracted to Christ by the way we live our lives, and the sort of people we are in the community? Jesus Himself was magnetic. He drew people to Him. As His Body on earth, shouldn't we be doing the same? And if we're not, what needs to happen in our midst to change the situation? Perhaps radical steps are needed to bring this about.

Seeking God

Led by Asa, the people renewed their covenant vows to the Lord, and made thousands of animal sacrifices as proof of their sincerity and wholehearted commitment to God. They vowed 'to seek the LORD, the God of their fathers, with all their heart and soul' (v.12), and put to death those who worshipped other gods, whoever they were. Typically, Asa again led the way in this by making an example of his own family. He 'deposed his grandmother Maacah from her position as queen mother, because she had made a repulsive Asherah pole' (v.16). Asa duly cut it down and burnt it.

The fact that Asa and the people of Judah were prepared to take such drastic measures as putting people to death shows that they realised how important it was to seek the Lord, to be united together in this common purpose, and not to tolerate idolatry in any of its forms. These people really meant business with God.

This raises some pointed questions for us today as God's people. How committed are we to God and to the work of His kingdom? Are we prepared to give of our time, money and talents sacrificially, to take up our cross and follow Him, to even die for Him? Are we united together in our service to God? Are we a team dedicated to Him, or a collection of individuals doing our own thing? Are we a people who seek the Lord, who focus on Him exclusively, who put Him at the centre of everything, who worship Him enthusiastically, who spend time with Him regularly, who ask Him for guidance and direction, who know His presence, peace and power with us? Are we really serious about our relationship with God?

As the people of Judah discovered (v.15), when we seek God with all our heart, soul, mind and strength, then we will surely find Him. Unlike a child in the game of hide-and-seek, God actually wants to be found by us (Deut. 4:29; Luke 11:10). He wants to walk with us, to talk with us, and to guide us; He wants us to know His presence with us every moment of the day. Jesus knew how important it was for all those who are His disciples to seek God, and urged them to make it their top priority (Matt. 6:33).

The problem of Ramah

The result of Asa and the nation seeking God was that the kingdom of Judah enjoyed twenty years of peace. Then, suddenly, in the thirty-sixth year of Asa's reign, something happened which unleashed a surprising chain of events (16:1–10).

Baasha had become king of Israel a couple of years after Asa's reign began in Judah, and there was a history of animosity between them. This came to a head when, after many years of mutual distrust but relatively peaceful co-existence, Baasha decided to fortify the town of Ramah. This act not only threatened the peace, but established a border control. This meant that Baasha could affect the economy of Judah by preventing traders from entering or leaving that country. Clearly, Asa could not allow this situation to continue. But, instead of seeking God about it, as we would have expected, given the events of his reign to date, Asa decided to take matters into his own hands.

Asa had brought into the Temple all the silver and gold and other articles taken as plunder from the battle with Jeroboam fought by his father, Abijah (see Chapter 17), along with the booty acquired when he himself had defeated the armies of Cush. All these items had been dedicated to God as sacred offerings by Asa. But he now used these very items to bribe Ben-Hadad, king of Aram (Syria), to break his treaty with Baasha, and restore the treaty between Judah and Aram made by their respective fathers. Ben-Hadad responded in just the way Asa had hoped he would by attacking Israel from the north, thus giving Baasha rather more urgent priorities than fortifying Ramah. While Baasha was thus preoccupied, Asa took the materials Baasha had brought to fortify Ramah to build up his own cities of Geba and Mizpah. It had all worked out rather well.

Rebuke

There is no doubt that, from a human perspective, Asa had dealt with the problem in a very politically astute way. But he had robbed God's Temple to do it, and had failed to seek the Lord about it. For some reason it seems that, over the years, Asa's reliance on God had waned. How could this have happened, given all the blessings Asa and Judah had received by seeking God? Perhaps it was because his own life and that of the nation had become so comfortable that he no longer felt the need to seek God as he had done previously. In my experience, it's easy to let our relationship with God slip when things are going well; so much so, that when difficulties then arise, we forget to seek God, and get ourselves in a mess.

Even though Asa seemed to have solved the problem of Ramah rather neatly, God was angry with him for the way he had gone about it. The next thing Asa knew, he was being berated by the prophet Hanani for relying on the king of Aram for the solution rather than on God. Hanani reminded Asa how he had sought the Lord when the Egyptians and Cushites invaded all those years ago, and how God had delivered him from them. If Asa had trusted in God, maintained the prophet, he would have achieved a better result, implying that the king of Aram would have been dealt with as well as Baasha. Hanani left Asa in no doubt that his actions showed his lack of commitment to God, describing what Asa had done by not relying on God as 'a foolish thing' (v.9), which would result in the nation being at war from then on.

Although it's not wrong to use our own acumen to solve the problems we face, isn't it always better to seek God about them as well? After all, does He not see the whole picture? And will He not guide us in the way we use our natural abilities, so that the problem will be sorted out in the best possible way?

A sad picture

How would Asa respond to Hanani's message? In years gone by, he would undoubtedly have been repentant and remorseful. But his reaction now was one of anger and fury. Asa had Hanani thrown into prison, a classic case of 'shooting' the messenger because he didn't like the contents of the message. Not only that, but 'At the same time Asa brutally oppressed some of the people' (v.10), an action which would have been unthinkable only a few years previously.

In acting like this, it seems that Asa was stubbornly trying to justify what he had done, rather than confessing his wrongdoing, admitting his failures, and asking God's forgiveness. Do we react in a similar way when God rebukes us? If so, then perhaps we need to remind ourselves that God only disciplines us because He loves us, and wants our relationship with Him to be restored (Heb. 12:5–11).

The sad decline in Asa's relationship with God is seen in the way he confronted problems, in the way he dealt with rebuke, and in the way he took his anger out on others. Three years later, Asa 'was afflicted with a disease in his feet' (v.12). Even though the disease was severe, he relied solely on the physicians of the day. Not once did Asa seek the Lord about it.

What a sad picture this presents of a king who, for the first thirty-five years of his reign, governed in an exemplary manner, but during the last six years of his rule slipped further and further away from God, until his relationship with God became almost non-existent. If we feel far away from God at this time, then guess who's moved! Unlike Asa, may we never lose the desire to seek the Lord with all our heart and with all our soul.

Chapter 19

A Puzzling Enigma

Jehoshaphat

2 Chronicles 17:1–21:1
(Other bit part players appearing: Ahab, Athaliah, Micaiah, Zedekiah, Jehu, Jahaziel, Ahaziah)

Religious education

After the death of his father, Asa (see Chapter 18), Jehoshaphat became the fourth king of Judah. He was thirty-five years old, and would rule the kingdom for twenty-five years. He made an immediate impact on the kingdom by strengthening it in two ways: militarily and spiritually. Jehoshaphat took measures to increase the security of the kingdom by stationing troops in all the fortified cities of Judah, and establishing garrisons in the towns along the northern border with Israel (17:1–2).

At the same time, Jehoshaphat was impacting the spiritual life of the nation. He continued the programme to destroy all vestiges of pagan worship begun by his father, and 'sought the God of his father and followed his commands … His heart was devoted to the ways of the LORD' (vv.4,6). Jehoshaphat decided that the people needed to undergo a programme of religious education. When Asa had ceased to 'seek the Lord' towards the end of his reign, so had the people. This meant that there was now considerable ignorance of God's laws. The people needed help, not only to comprehend these laws, but also to understand how to worship God, and how important it was to obey these laws in their daily lives.

To accomplish this, Jehoshaphat set up teaching teams composed of officials, Levites and priests to tour the kingdom and hold a series of seminars, at which the people would be taught about these matters (vv.7–9). The result was that Judah turned back to God, and the impact of this was felt in the nations around them: 'the fear of the LORD fell on all the kingdoms of the lands surrounding Judah' (v.10). Not only did Judah experience a time of peace because of this, but the neighbouring kingdoms sent tribute and goods to Jehoshaphat to cement their relationships with him, thus strengthening his position in the region (vv.11–13).

Is it not just as important for our churches to provide their congregations with a good grounding in the Word of God through systematic Bible teaching for the adults, and enjoyable Bible-based activities for the children and young people, with an understanding of how to apply what the Bible teaches to our lives? Churches that do this are usually exciting places to be, and often make a powerful impact on the people around them, as Judah did. Wouldn't it be wonderful if every community where there is a church became aware of the awesomeness, power and love of God through the holy living, good works, loving attitudes and obedience to God of its congregation?

An unholy alliance

What happened next is indicative of Jehoshaphat's enigmatic personality. Having become powerful and prosperous by doing all the right things, Jehoshaphat now took an extraordinary decision: to make an alliance with Ahab, the wicked and cunning king of Israel. How could he possibly even contemplate such an unholy alliance? A righteous man of God teaming up with an evil worshipper of Baal! Jehoshaphat had absolutely no need to do this. He had far more to lose than to gain by it, as events would prove. Ahab, on the other hand, had much to gain by this alliance, which would not only secure his southern border and allow him to focus his defences against Syria to the north, but would also allow him to benefit from Judah's prosperity through trade, and make the military forces of Judah available to him.

In making a treaty with Israel, Jehoshaphat was departing from the policy adopted by all his predecessors, who believed Judah should remain totally separated from Israel. As has often been the case between allied nations, the agreement was sealed by a royal marriage. Jehoshaphat married his son and successor, Jehoram, to Athaliah, the daughter of Ahab and Jezebel. This would prove to be a very big mistake, and bring nothing but trouble. Athaliah was as God-defying and strident as her mother, not to mention as cunning as her father, and would become Judah's worst nightmare. She brought the worship of Baal and all the evil practices associated with it into Judah, and soon had Jehoram under her spell.

Jehoshaphat didn't consult God before embarking on this fateful alliance, and choosing a wife for his son. Do we ask God for guidance in choosing our friends and, more importantly, our marriage partners? The Bible warns us about becoming closely involved with non-believers (2 Cor. 6:14). Do we heed the warning?

To war or not to war

It wasn't long before Ahab was persuading Jehoshaphat to enter with him into an ill-advised war with Ahab's longstanding enemy Syria, known then as Aram. Ahab invited Jehoshaphat to stay with him at his palace in Samaria, the capital city. Ahab proceeded to make a great fuss of him, before asking Jehoshaphat if he would join him in seeking to recapture Ramoth Gilead, which had fallen into Syrian hands some years before.

Jehoshaphat's reply was astonishing: 'I am as you are, and my people as your people; we will join you in the war' (18:3). Perhaps this throws some light on Jehoshaphat's motives for agreeing to this alliance in the first place. Maybe he was idealistic or naive enough to think that he could influence Israel for the good, even if it did mean having to ignore the differences between them. This is often the reason given for having close relationships with non-believers but, in my experience, it rarely works. Indeed, the opposite is usually the outcome.

Interestingly, in spite of the fact that what he had done was displeasing to God, Jehoshaphat insisted on seeking 'the counsel of the LORD' (v.4) about this matter. It didn't seem to occur to Jehoshaphat that, having angered God by making this alliance, he ought to be asking God's forgiveness, never mind His help. But, once again, God would be gracious and merciful to an errant king, and give Jehoshaphat the benefit of His counsel through the prophet Micaiah.

Ahab knew what the prophets they consulted would say, since they were all hand-picked 'yes-men', who would always tell Ahab what he wanted to hear. Surprise, surprise, when asked whether Ramoth Gilead should be attacked, all 400 of Ahab's prophets were distinctly 'on message', and answered as one, 'Go … for God will give it into the king's hand' (v.5).

Under pressure

Jehoshaphat remained unconvinced by this, especially since these 400 prophets worshipped the Lord Baal and not the Lord God. So he asked Ahab, 'Is there not a prophet of the LORD here whom we can enquire of?' (v.6). Ahab reluctantly conceded that there was one such individual remaining in his kingdom whose name was Micaiah, adding, 'but I hate him because he never prophesies anything good about me, but always bad' (v.7).

As Ahab and Jehoshaphat sat enthroned in majesty, wearing their royal robes, Ahab's prophets continued to prophesy that they should go to war. One of them, Zedekiah, even had a visual aid to make his point! He held aloft the iron horns he had made, declaring, 'This is what the LORD says: "With these you will gore the Arameans until they are destroyed"' (v.10). Micaiah was placed under severe pressure to conform by the messenger sent to get him, but he maintained that he would speak out what the Lord gave him to say (vv.12–13).

However, when he arrived and heard what all the other prophets were saying, Micaiah must have really felt the pressure, because he said the same thing as all the others when asked the question by Ahab. Unconvinced by the truth of his answer, presumably because Micaiah never ever said the same as the others, Ahab told him, 'How many times must I make you swear to tell me nothing but the truth in the name of the LORD?' (v.15). Then Micaiah gave it to them straight, saying that all the other prophets were lying, and that they should all just go home in peace, otherwise disaster would overtake them, and Ahab himself would be killed in battle (vv.16–22).

On hearing this, Ahab leant across to Jehoshaphat and hissed ruefully, 'Didn't I tell you that he never prophesies anything good about me, but only bad?' (v.17). Zedekiah was so enraged by what Micaiah had said that he slapped him across the face for his pains (v.23). But Micaiah maintained that it was he who had told the truth. As he was dragged off to prison at Ahab's command, to be fed only on bread and water until the king returned safely, Micaiah shouted at Ahab, 'If you ever return safely, the LORD has not spoken through me' (v.27).

As both Micaiah and Simon Peter found, there are times when we all feel the pressure to go along with the crowd for fear of standing out and being ridiculed for what we believe, however loyal we may think we are to God (Luke 22:54–62). Standing up for what we know to be right isn't always easy; but isn't it better to do what is right in God's sight, even though we may have to face unpleasant consequences (Matt. 5:11–12)? After all, isn't this one of the costs of discipleship?

Dichotomy of thinking

Once again we see the enigma that was Jehoshaphat. Having heard God's counsel through Micaiah, he chose to ignore it completely. All those years of success achieved by depending on God and obeying Him suddenly seemed to count for nothing in his mind. Yet, how often do we act in the very same way as Jehoshaphat, and show a similar dichotomy in our thinking? Is it not true that there are times in our lives when we are happy to trust God and depend on Him, but then at other times we totally ignore what He says for some reason, or even fail to consult Him at all?

Maybe it's to do with how serious we consider the situation to be. If that is so, then perhaps we need to remind ourselves that God is just as interested in the everyday, nitty-gritty problems that we face as He is in the large and difficult ones. And is it not just as important for us to bring to God the matters we think we can cope with or decide about for ourselves, so that we have His wisdom and avoid making costly mistakes? For some reason, Jehoshaphat didn't do this when faced with what he seems to have considered minor matters, and he must have spent the rest of his life regretting his mistakes. Unfortunately, he didn't always seem to learn from them, though. Do we?

A cunning plan

Instead of returning home, as Micaiah had counselled him to do, Jehoshaphat foolishly decided to go into battle with his new-found friend and ally. Meanwhile, in keeping with his character, Ahab had devised a cunning plan to make sure that Micaiah's prophecy could not possibly come to pass.

Ahab's plan was this: rather than wearing his royal robes, he would go into battle in disguise, kitted out as an ordinary soldier. Jehoshaphat, on the other hand, was to wear his royal robes (v.29). This would, in fact, draw fire from the Syrians towards Jehoshaphat, as they were bound to think they were aiming at the king of Israel, not realising he was the king of Judah. Was it part of Ahab's cunning plan to have Jehoshaphat killed in the battle, which Ahab himself fully intended to survive? Then with his daughter, Athaliah, as queen of Judah, the doors of the southern kingdom would be open to him.

Clearly, Jehoshaphat had no such suspicions, and happily went along with Ahab's plan. If Jehoshaphat didn't realise the inevitable consequences of parading into action wearing his royal robes before battle commenced, he soon became aware of the peril he was in once the fighting began. The king of Syria (Aram) was determined to slay Ahab, and told his chariot commanders to focus their attack on him. So when they saw Jehoshaphat, they assumed he was the king of Israel, and turned to attack him (vv.30–31).

Realising what was happening, Jehoshaphat knew he was in serious trouble, so he cried out to the Lord. In spite of his anger, God was merciful to Jehoshaphat, and responded to his cry: 'God drew them away from him, for when the chariot commanders saw that he was not the king of Israel, they stopped pursuing him' (v.32).

By 'chance'

Meanwhile, Ahab's cunning survival plan was going so well, until 'someone drew his bow at random and hit the king of Israel between the sections of his armour' (v.33). By sheer 'chance', an arrow came flying his way which didn't bounce off his armour, but hit Ahab in the body between two of its sections. He survived for a while, but finally died at sunset (v.34).

God's word concerning the king of Israel was fulfilled, despite Ahab's attempts to avoid it happening, and despite the fact that his executioner never knew what he had done. Ahab thought he was being so clever, but he couldn't outsmart God. This serves as yet another reminder that what God has purposed will inevitably come to pass, no matter what people may do to try and prevent it. God's plans can never be thwarted by people.

Legal reorganisation

Jehoshaphat escaped from the battle, and returned home safely to his palace in Jerusalem. On the way he was met by the prophet Jehu, who was sent by God to make a few salient points to Jehoshaphat concerning the way he had acted. Jehu told the king in no uncertain terms that he had been totally lacking in discernment: 'Should you help the wicked and love those who hate the LORD?' (19:2). No prizes for guessing whom the prophet had in mind! But, although Jehoshaphat's ill-judged alliance had angered him, on balance the Lord still saw more good than bad in him, 'for you have rid the land of the Asherah poles and have set your heart on seeking God' (v.3).

To his credit, Jehoshaphat responded positively to what God had said through the prophet. Indeed, this enigmatic man seems to have reverted to his original God-honouring ways. He embarked on a royal tour of the whole kingdom, appointing men to be judges in each city as he visited it. He also appointed officials in Jerusalem to help to administer the law of the Lord and to rule in civil matters. Such a system and structure was unprecedented in the legal history of the kingdom, and reorganised the judiciary completely.

Jehoshaphat gave these judges and officials very clear instructions: 'Consider carefully what you do, because you are not judging for man but for the LORD, who is with you whenever you give a verdict. Now let the fear of the LORD be upon you. Judge carefully, for with the LORD ... there is no injustice or partiality or bribery ... You must serve faithfully and wholeheartedly ... Act with courage' (vv.6–7,9,11). Are not these wise words just as helpful and applicable to all those of us in positions of responsibility today?

Fasting

Some time later, Judah was about to be invaded by the massed forces of Moab and Ammon (see Chapter 1). Vastly outnumbered, Jehoshaphat knew he was facing a national crisis. Perhaps he remembered a similar situation faced by his father Asa when the

Egyptians invaded (see Chapter 18). As usual when he realised that the situation was serious, Jehoshaphat did the right thing, and 'resolved to enquire of the LORD' (20:3). Because it was a national crisis, Jehoshaphat involved the whole nation, and 'proclaimed a fast for all Judah' (v.3); and the people responded magnificently, coming from every town in Judah to seek the Lord together.

It seems to me that God's people have largely forgotten the importance of fasting when seeking God's face over an important issue. Fasting enables us to spend more time in prayer and meditation. In my experience, that extra time spent in God's presence often serves to sharpen our spiritual awareness and to heighten our spiritual faculties, so that we become more conscious of God's presence and His leading in our lives.

Fasting involves going without food, some would say without liquid as well, for a period of time. Such physical self-denial is also a way of showing God, not to mention ourselves, that we really do mean business about the particular problem we are praying earnestly about at the moment. This may be a personal matter. It may be something to do with the church, such as what to do about a difficult situation, or whether to embark on a particular project. In my experience, fasting together as God's people often results in the way forward being made clear.

The king's prayer

Jehoshaphat then went to the Temple to lead the vast crowd, tightly packed and thronged together as they were, in prayer (vv.6–12). Maybe he was inspired by the memory of what his father had said when faced by the Egyptian threat. The focus of both their prayers was the same: the power and sovereignty of God. Jehoshaphat began by remembering God's mighty acts in the past, and how He had caused the building of the Temple where His name was to be worshipped. Then he expressed his faith in God, believing that He would hear their cry and save them from the invaders. Finally, Jehoshaphat handed the situation over to God, acknowledging that their salvation lay entirely in His hands, because they were powerless to save themselves.

Like the prayer of Asa, Jehoshaphat's prayer also gives us a good framework for our own. To start by affirming God's power and sovereignty reminds us that nothing is impossible for God to do, and helps us to get our problems into perspective. To then remind ourselves of what God has already done encourages us to express our faith and belief that God will hear our prayer, and will deal with our current problem. Acknowledging our weakness and putting the matter into God's hands signals our submission to God's will. As Jehoshaphat so beautifully put it: 'We do not know what to do, but our eyes are upon you' (v.12).

Imagine the hush that must have descended upon the crowd as Jehoshaphat completed his prayer, and 'All the men of Judah, with their wives and children and little ones, stood there before the LORD' (v.13), waiting expectantly. What an amazing picture those words conjure up! God's people packed together against the backdrop of the magnificent Temple, standing before almighty God; the expectant hush hiding the fears of those thousands of families for their safety, and that of their children, in view of the impending invasion. Would they experience death, or deliverance?

God speaks

Suddenly, a voice broke through the silence, as Jahaziel spoke to the assembled multitude under the anointing of the Spirit of the Lord (vv.14–17). God's message through Jahaziel was one of encouragement and instruction: 'Do not be afraid or discouraged because of this vast army. For the battle is not yours, but God's. Tomorrow march down against them ... You will not have to fight this battle. Take up your positions; stand firm and see the deliverance the LORD will give you ... Go out to face them tomorrow, and the LORD will be with you.' It must have taken a lot of courage for Jahaziel to speak out God's word to the people. And God is still looking for courageous men and women today who will speak out His truth with boldness.

The response of the people to God's word was one of faith, trust, belief and obedience. Jehoshaphat led the people in bowing down before the Lord as an act of submission, and in worshipping Him. This was followed by a time of vibrant praise led by some of the Levites.

The power of praise

The next morning, Jehoshaphat encouraged the people to stand firm in their faith. Then Jehoshaphat did something quite extraordinary. He gathered together a male voice choir, and told them not only to sing praise to the Lord, but to do so while going out on to the battlefield in front of the army. They were to lead the troops into battle while singing 'Give thanks to the LORD, for his love endures for ever' (v.21).

What courage it must have taken them to do this. Imagine being a member of that choir! They could have protested that they were singers not soldiers. But, although they were undoubtedly full of trepidation, they summoned up their faith, and set off in the direction of the enemy, singing praises to God in the loudest voices they could muster. And 'As they began to sing and praise' (v.22), the Lord began to do His work to bring about the destruction of their enemies, who began fighting among themselves.

So when the singers and the army came within sight of the enemy, 'they saw only dead bodies lying on the ground; no-one had escaped' (v.24). They must have stopped and stared in astonishment at the scene laid out before them. God had been true to His promise. There was so much plunder it took three days to collect it. On the fourth day, they assembled in the valley of Beracah, which means 'praise', to do exactly that. From there, they returned to Jerusalem full of joy and rejoicing at what God had done, and continued to praise God in the Temple, accompanied by harps, lutes and trumpets (vv.25–28).

The result of this amazing demonstration of God's power was

that the 'fear of God' came upon all the nations around Judah, and 'the kingdom of Jehoshaphat was at peace' (vv.29–30). Jehoshaphat's reign had come full circle; he now found himself in exactly the same position he had experienced in the early years of his reign (17:10), before he decided he could manage without relying on God. Had he learnt his lesson at last?

Praise was the key to this victory. It was praise that released the power of God to meet the needs of the people of God. Do we praise God when we're in a battle, be it personally or as a Church? This incident encourages us to give our battle to God, because although we are powerless, He is powerful – so it's His battle, not ours. Our part is to believe in faith, and to praise God with all our heart, even though praising God is the last thing we may feel like doing, in the expectation that God's power will be released into our situation or circumstances. Paul and Silas did exactly that, and look what happened to them (Acts 16:25–34).

Déjà vu

Sadly, Jehoshaphat still hadn't learnt his lesson. Unbelievably, this enigmatic king entered into another unwise alliance with, of all people, Ahab's son, Ahaziah – not to be confused with Jehoshaphat's grandson of the same name, the son of Jehoram and Athaliah. Ahaziah was now king of Israel. Without consulting God, Jehoshaphat decided to go into a business venture with him, building a fleet of trading ships (vv.35–37). God sent a prophet named Eliezer to tell Jehoshaphat that, because he had allied himself with Ahaziah, who was as bad as his father had been, God would scupper their plans. Sure enough, 'The ships were wrecked and were not able to set sail to trade' (v.37).

Ahaziah died soon afterwards, and was succeeded by his brother, Joram. Towards the end of his reign, Jehoshaphat allowed Joram to pass through Judah on his way to fight the Moabites with the words, 'I will go with you ... I am as you are, my people as your people' (2 Kings 3:7). Now where have we heard those words before?

Chapter 20

An Eye to the Main Chance

Gehazi

2 Kings 4:1–5:27

(Other bit part players appearing: the Shunammite woman, Naaman)

The room on the roof

When the prophet Elisha began his ministry, Joram, a son of Ahab (see Chapter 19), was the king of Israel. Gehazi was Elisha's servant, and would have the privilege of seeing God at work in many miraculous ways throughout his master's ministry, which continued during the reigns of Jehu, Jehoahaz and Jehoash.

Gehazi played a part in two of these miracles. The first involved the son of a wealthy Shunammite woman. This particular lady and her husband realised that Elisha was a prophet of God, and wanted to support him in his ministry. So, on her initiative, they made a small room on the roof of their house in which they put a bed, a table, a chair and a lamp for Elisha's exclusive use whenever he came to Shunem (4:9–10). In what practical and sacrificial ways do we support and help those who are in full-time ministry for God?

203

Elisha knew that this couple were not supporting him for any personal gain. They were giving selflessly, and expecting nothing in return (see Acts 20:35). So, one day, Elisha told Gehazi to bring the Shunammite woman to him. Elisha then proceeded to ask her whether he could do anything for her in return, such as drop a word in royal or military circles (v.13). This indicates that, unlike his predecessor Elijah, Elisha's input was welcomed at court and in the affairs of the nation.

The Shunammite's son

His hostess replied that she was quite content, but Elisha was determined to repay her kindness in some way. The fact that he asked Gehazi about it shows that he valued his servant's opinion, and that they had a good relationship. Gehazi replied that the only thing she was lacking was a son, and she was never likely to have one, because her husband was old (v.14). Immediately, Elisha summoned her, and promised her that 'About this time next year … you will hold a son in your arms' (v.16). Not surprisingly, she didn't believe what Elisha had said, but it came to pass just as the prophet had foretold.

Some years later, the boy complained of a bad headache, and died soon afterwards in his mother's arms. What she did next shows that she must have had the faith to believe that a miracle was possible for her son. She carried his lifeless body up to the room on the roof, and laid her son on *Elisha's* bed, not on his own. Then she set off in the direction of Mount Carmel to find Elisha as fast as the donkey would carry her (vv.18–25).

Seeing her in the distance, Elisha sent Gehazi to find out if there was a problem, to which she replied, 'Everything is all right' (v.26). How often do we mouth the same words when everything is far from all right? Maybe it's because we don't want people to think that we can't cope, or we assume that they're too busy to help us. Perhaps we need to overcome our pride, and what may be wrong assumptions, and allow others the opportunity to minister to us. Or perhaps we say such things because we know that there's nothing they can do, so we don't see the point in burdening them with our troubles. But shouldn't we at least allow people the opportunity to pray with us and for us?

Desperation and disappointment

The Shunammite fobbed Gehazi off with these words only because she wanted to get to speak to the man of God as quickly as possible. Shouldn't crying out to God always be the first thing we do, because He is always the One who can meet our needs? But, in my experience, it's often not what we do first. In her desperation, she flung herself down on the ground, grabbed hold of Elisha's feet, and began to sob out her distress. Thank God that He is always there to cling on to, and to sob our hearts out to, in the desperate times we experience.

Gehazi tried to push her away, presumably because he felt that such a public display by the woman was somehow demeaning to his master. Elisha rebuked Gehazi for such insensitivity, and told him to run as fast as he could to the Shunammite's house, taking the prophet's staff with him, and not to allow himself to be distracted by anyone on the way. When he got there, Gehazi was to lay Elisha's staff on the boy's face. In the meantime, Elisha would follow on behind with the boy's mother (vv.27–30).

Gehazi must have been very excited at the prospect of seeing a miracle happen before his very eyes. He followed his master's instructions to the letter, but the expected miracle did not take place: there was no response from the boy. How disappointed Gehazi must have been as he relayed the news to his master and the boy's mother as they approached the house (v.31).

Alive again

Gehazi must also have been very disappointed at what happened next. Elisha went into the room with the boy, shutting both him and the boy's mother outside. Did Gehazi ever find out what happened in that room? Did Elisha tell Gehazi how he had stretched himself out face down on top of the boy twice, and how the boy had then sneezed seven times before opening his eyes (vv.32–35)?

In my experience, we don't always see how God works things out, but we can nevertheless see that His hand has been at work, as Gehazi was about to. Gehazi must have hung around outside, wondering what was going on. Then, suddenly, he heard his master's voice summoning him. On entering the room, he saw the boy alive again, and went to fetch his mother, whose joy can only be imagined (vv.36–37).

There is an interesting postscript to this incident. Elisha advised the Shunammite and her husband to leave the area because a famine was imminent. In fact, they lived among the Philistines for seven years. When they returned, it was Gehazi who pleaded with the king of Israel on their behalf to have their land restored to them (vv.1–6). This is another example of how well thought of Elisha and Gehazi were in the court of the kings of Israel.

The feeding of one hundred men

The second miracle in which Gehazi played his part in some ways foreshadowed the time when Jesus would feed five thousand men (Mark 6:30–44). However, rather than five thousand there were only a hundred, and they were fed with twenty loaves of bread rather than five loaves and two fish (v.42). But even so, it was undoubtedly a miraculous event.

Not surprisingly, Gehazi questioned Elisha's instructions for him to feed the one hundred men gathered with them with the twenty loaves which had been brought, saying, 'How can I set this before a hundred men?' (v.43). But Elisha commanded him to proceed on the authority of what God had told him: 'They will eat and have some left over' (v.43). And so it was that the men ate their fill, and there was bread left uneaten – another example of seeing God's hand at work without knowing quite how He's worked it!

But it is for what happened in the aftermath of a miracle in which he played no part that Gehazi is most remembered.

A little girl's faith

Just for a change, Israel and its much stronger, big-bully neighbour to the north-east, Syria (Aram), were at peace. Then, out of the blue, Naaman, the commander-in-chief of the Syrian army, arrived in the capital city of Israel with his retinue, bringing a letter from his king that read: 'With this letter I am sending my servant Naaman to you so that you may cure him of his leprosy' (5:6).

The king of Israel was beside himself with fear, seeing this as a ruse by the Syrian king to pick a fight with him, and justify yet another series of raids on Israel. Little did he know that Naaman had come at the suggestion of his wife's young Israeli servant girl to seek out the prophet whom the girl maintained could cure him of his affliction. What a tribute this is to that little girl, and what an example she is to all of us: captured, separated from her parents, forced into servitude, frightened and alone in a foreign land, she remained faithful to her God, and spoke up boldly when the opportunity presented itself in the situation where she found herself (v.3). And because of her faith in God, her master would not only experience physical healing, but come to faith in her God too (vv.15,17–18). May we all have the same courage to speak out boldly when we have the chance, whatever the situation we find ourselves in.

An auspicious visitor

On hearing of the king's predicament, Elisha sent a message telling the king to send Naaman to him. Whether it was Gehazi who took the message or not, Elisha's servant would certainly have been aware of Naaman's arrival at his master's door, complete with soldiers, horses and chariots. Gehazi would undoubtedly have been amazed that Elisha didn't even go to the door to welcome such an auspicious visitor. The man of God merely sent Gehazi, or another of his servants, to the mighty Naaman with a message telling the Syrian to 'Go, wash yourself seven times in the Jordan, and your flesh will be restored and you will be cleansed' (v.10). Whoever delivered that message must have done so in fear and trepidation!

Naaman was distinctly unimpressed by the fact that Elisha hadn't even done him the courtesy of showing his face, not to mention being told to go and wash in the relatively unpleasant waters of the Jordan. However, his men managed to coax Naaman out of his rage and into the River Jordan, where he obeyed the prophet's instructions and was duly cleansed of his leprosy.

The next thing Gehazi knew – if he didn't actually follow the party down to the Jordan at a discreet distance to see what happened – was that Naaman was knocking on his master's door again. This time, Elisha did go out to meet him, and was offered a gift by the grateful Syrian, which he refused, despite Naaman's pleas. Shortly afterwards, Naaman set off on his journey home.

The eyes have it

Gehazi, who had undoubtedly seen and heard all that had taken place, came to his own conclusion and decision: 'My master was too easy on Naaman, this Aramean, by not accepting from him what he brought. As surely as the LORD lives, I will run after him and get something from him' (v.20). His eyes must have bulged as he saw the gifts Naaman was offering Elisha. 'What harm could it possibly do to have a slice of that?' he must have thought to himself. 'No one need ever know!' His greed would inevitably lead to deception.

When Naaman noticed Gehazi running after him, he got down from his chariot to find out if everything was all right. Gehazi assured him that it was, but made up a story about some needy prophets having just arrived, and could Naaman possibly see his way clear to helping out? Naaman gladly obliged, giving Gehazi so much stuff that it needed two of Naaman's servants to help carry it all. When home was in sight, Gehazi sent the servants away (vv.21–24). He then must have made at least two journeys back and forth to the place where he had hidden the bounty to get it all back to the house.

Bearing the marks

With everything safely stashed away, Gehazi went to see if Elisha required anything. Elisha then asked him what for me is one of the most chilling questions in the whole of the Bible: 'Where have you been, Gehazi?' (v.25). It seems that Elisha was giving his servant the chance to confess his wrongdoing. Unfortunately, Gehazi didn't take it, and lied brazenly, 'Your servant didn't go anywhere' (v.25). We can only imagine the withering look Elisha must have given his servant as he said, 'Was not my spirit with you when the man got down from his chariot to meet you? Is this the time to take money, or to accept clothes ...?' (v.26).

When faced with our sin, do we confess it to God and receive His forgiveness, or deny it and put ourselves under His judgment? The consequences for Gehazi, and his family too, were dire. Elisha dramatically pronounced Gehazi's chilling fate: '"Naaman's leprosy will cling to you and to your descendants for ever." Then Gehazi went from Elisha's presence and he was leprous, as white as snow' (v.27).

This good servant of Elisha, who was well thought of by the royal court, as well as by the prophet, had succumbed to one moment of temptation, and let himself down badly. But it seems to me that his greater mistake was not to repent when given the opportunity. If only he'd confessed when challenged, the judgment upon him would undoubtedly have been very different. As it was, Gehazi had to live the rest of his life bearing the marks and suffering the consequences of his sinfulness. However, it seems that the form of leprosy he carried was not contagious, because apparently he continued to serve Elisha (8:1–6) – another example of God's mercy?

Isn't it wonderful to know that God's blessings and gifts cannot be bought? He gives them freely out of the abundance of His grace (Eph. 2:7–8). How could we possibly repay God for His gift of salvation, not to mention all the other blessings He showers upon us? Gehazi needed to understand this, as well as the fact that true service to God is born of love and devotion, and seeks no personal gain, be it in the form of people's praise or material reward. Are our eyes focused on the main chance, or on serving our heavenly Master? Do our lives bear the marks of devoted service to our Lord and Saviour?

Chapter 21

The Zealous Crusader

Jehu

2 Kings 9–10
(Other bit part players appearing: Joram, Ahaziah,
Jezebel, Jehonadab)

The anointing

Once again, the kingdom of Israel was at war with Syria (Aram). Joram, the king of Israel, supported by his nephew, Ahaziah, the king of Judah, was engaged in battle with the Syrians at Ramoth Gilead. The commander of the army of Israel was Jehu. During the battle, Joram was wounded, and withdrew to the city of Jezreel to recover from his injuries, leaving Jehu in charge. Ahaziah also went to Jezreel to be with his uncle (8:28–29).

During the reign of Joram's father, Ahab, Elijah had anointed Jehu as a future king of Israel, who would bring God's judgment upon that kingdom (1 Kings 19:15–17). Elisha, who had been anointed around the same time, would have known about this. With Joram wounded, Elisha decided that this was the time for Jehu to take over the kingdom, and be officially anointed king in

Joram's place.

Elisha summoned one of the prophets, and gave him strict instructions with regard to Jehu's anointing: it was to be done privately, and Jehu was to be given God's authorisation to destroy the house of Ahab, thus avenging the slaughter of God's servants and prophets carried out by Ahab's wife, Jezebel, who one day would be devoured by dogs. After carrying out the anointing, the prophet was to get out of there as fast as his legs would carry him before the massacre began. The prophet followed Elisha's instructions to the letter (9:1–10).

When Jehu's fellow-officers saw the prophet sprinting off into the distance after his private meeting with Jehu, they asked him, 'Is everything all right? Why did this madman come to you?' (v.11). When Jehu had finished telling them all that had occurred, the officers blew a trumpet and proclaimed Jehu as king, even though Joram was still alive and well.

The crusade begins

Jehu lost no time in embarking on his God-given crusade to purge the land of the house of Ahab. Jehu knew that the first person to get rid of was Joram. So that Joram wouldn't get wind of what was going on, Jehu made sure that no one could leave Ramoth Gilead and take the news to Jezreel, thus alerting Joram. Taking a detachment of troops with him, Jehu set off for Jezreel in his chariot. Seeing the troops in the distance, Joram sent out messengers to find out who they were, and if their intentions were peaceful, but neither of them returned, having decided to join Jehu.

They say you can tell a lot about a person from the way that they drive! This was certainly true of Jehu, whose driving style was legendary for its recklessness. Indeed, this was how the lookout standing on the tower in Jezreel was able to identify that it was Jehu who was approaching the city: 'The driving is like that of Jehu son of Nimshi – he drives like a madman' (v.20). Hearing that it was his commander coming, Joram decided to ride out to meet him, accompanied by his nephew Ahaziah, both in their own chariots.

Significantly, they met at the plot of ground that had once belonged to a man called Naboth, a local citizen. Joram's parents, Ahab and Jezebel, had illegally acquired this property after Jezebel plotted the murder of Naboth because he refused to sell his family vineyard to them (1 Kings 21:1–24). Elijah had prophesied that 'In the place where dogs licked up Naboth's blood, dogs will lick up your blood – yes, yours!' That prophecy was about to be fulfilled in the death of Ahab's son.

Shot trying to escape

When Joram tentatively asked Jehu if he had 'come in peace', Jehu replied, 'How can there be peace ... as long as all the idolatry and witchcraft of your mother Jezebel abound?' (v.22). Clearly, Jehu saw his crusade as more than just eliminating the house of Ahab; the land was also to be cleansed of the worship of Baal, which Jezebel had introduced, and everything associated with it. The house of Ahab and the worship of Baal were inextricably intertwined; they were a cancer in the kingdom of Israel, and had to be dealt with drastically. However, in his zeal to accomplish his God-given mission, there is no doubt that Jehu showed a recklessness and a callousness that was over the top and uncalled for.

Jehu's reply left Joram in no doubt that his days were numbered. As Joram tried to escape in his chariot, shouting 'Treachery, Ahaziah!' (v.23), Jehu shot an arrow into his back between the shoulders, piercing his heart. Jehu clearly knew about Elijah's prophecy, as he ordered Joram's body to be thrown 'on the field that belonged to Naboth the Jezreelite' (v.25). But Jehu seems to have expanded it to justify his callous treatment of Joram's body (v.26).

Meanwhile, Ahaziah tried to make good his escape, but Jehu's men chased after him and severely wounded him. Ahaziah made it as far as Megiddo, where he died. To kill the king of Judah was not commanded by the prophet. Presumably Jehu's justification for such an act was that Ahaziah was a grandson of Ahab. The zealous crusader was beginning to interpret God's briefing in his own way.

Are we inclined to do something similar? Do we ever twist, take out of context, or misinterpret God's Word to make it fit in with what we want it to say in order to justify our actions?

Jezebel's demise

Next on Jehu's list was Jezebel. Defiant to the last, Jezebel put on her make-up and did her hair. If she was going to die, she was going to do it in style! Jezebel watched out of her upper floor window in the palace as Jehu entered Jezreel. The news of her son's death must have already reached her because she leant out of the window and shouted ironically at Jehu, 'Have you come in peace, Zimri, you murderer of your master?' (v.31). Zimri was an army commander who had committed treason in the past by killing Elah and then proclaiming himself king (1 Kings 16:8–10). As far as Jezebel was concerned, Jehu, another army commander, was guilty of exactly the same crime.

Jehu wasn't going to take any lectures from Jezebel about how to behave. He persuaded some men standing near Jezebel that, if they were on his side, they should show their allegiance by grabbing her and throwing her down. Realising which way the wind was now blowing, they obliged, with the result that Jezebel hit the ground, and was then deliberately trampled underfoot by Jehu's horses, probably unnecessarily, spattering blood everywhere.

The fact that Jehu went and had a meal leaving Jezebel's body lying in the street could be seen as another example of callousness. However, he did send men to bury Jezebel later, but all that was left of her by then was her skull, feet and hands: the dogs had consumed the rest, in accordance with Elijah's prophecy about her death in the wake of the Naboth scandal (1 Kings 21:23). Again,

Jehu expanded the prophecy, seemingly to justify his treatment of her (v.37).

Heads in baskets

Jehu knew that there were still seventy sons of the house of Ahab living back in Samaria. Jehu's proposal to the leaders of the city and the guardians of these princes was that they should set one of them up as a rival king so that the matter could be sorted in battle. Realising they stood no chance, they agreed to do anything Jehu asked.

So Jehu wrote them a second letter, which he cleverly worded to be capable of two interpretations: 'If you are on my side and will obey me, take the heads of your master's sons and come to me in Jezreel by this time tomorrow' (10:6). As Jehu had undoubtedly hoped, they took his message literally. Rather than bringing the princes to meet him, they slaughtered all seventy of them, sending their heads to Jehu in baskets. Thus Jehu had achieved his purpose, but in a way which meant no blame could be attached to him for their deaths.

But that was by no means the end of Jehu's bloodbath. In his zealousness he further exceeded God's commands by proceeding to slaughter all those in any way remotely connected to the house of Ahab, along with forty-two relatives of Ahaziah who had arrived from Judah (vv.11–14). Many years later, God pronounced punishment on the house of Jehu for his 'massacre at Jezreel', which would ultimately result in the end of the kingdom of Israel (Hosea 1:4–5).

History is littered with examples of revolutionary leaders who, like Jehu, in their fervour to get rid of the evils which existed, only succeeded in committing atrocities of their own, often justifying their actions with the claim that God was on their side.

'Zeal for the LORD'

Jehu actually boasted to a man named Jehonadab that he was doing all this out of his 'zeal for the LORD' (v.16). Interestingly, Jehonadab was also full of zeal for the Lord, but he showed it in a completely different way. Jehonadab separated his clan as far as possible from worldly involvement so they could live pure lives before God. They became known as the Recabites, named after Jehonadab's father, and they impressed God by their devotion to him (Jer. 35). So why did a man like Jehonadab throw in his lot with a man like Jehu? Mainly because it seems he also hated the worship of Baal, and wanted to see it destroyed.

The Bible actually encourages us to have zeal for the Lord. For example, Paul exhorts us: 'Never be lacking in zeal, but keep your spiritual fervour, serving the Lord' (Rom. 12:11). Jesus Himself was full of zeal. In a prophecy about Him, Isaiah speaks of Jesus as having 'wrapped himself in zeal as in a cloak' (Isa. 59:17). When Jesus cleansed the Temple, the disciples remembered that it was said of Him, 'Zeal for your house will consume me' (John 2:17).

However, unlike Jehu, the zeal that Jesus showed throughout His life was always under control, and never got out of hand or overstepped the mark. In my experience, this is rarely an issue that the Church has to confront. A lack of zeal tends to be more of a problem! When God looks at us, does He see a people who are full of ardent and fervent enthusiasm for the work of the kingdom, or, like the word itself, is zeal largely a forgotten concept among us? May God give us all a zeal for souls like Paul had, and a zeal to serve others like Epaphras did (1 Cor. 9:22; Col. 4:13, AV).

With Jehonadab in tow, Jehu summoned an assembly of all the prophets, ministers and servants of Baal, purporting to be an enthusiastic servant of Baal himself (vv.18–22). Jehu surrounded the temple where they were gathered with eighty armed men. At his signal, they entered the temple and systematically massacred all those inside, before demolishing the temple completely. The ruins of the temple became used as a toilet (10:23–27). The worship of Baal as well as the house of Ahab had now been destroyed.

Commendation and condemnation

It would be easy, but in my view unfair, to dismiss Jehu as nothing more than a bloodthirsty thug. True, there was a certain degree of callousness in the way he treated the bodies of Joram and Jezebel, but he probably felt justified in doing so, considering the havoc the house of Ahab had wrought in the kingdom of Israel. It is also true to say that he was overzealous at times in his 'zeal for the Lord'; but he was commended for carrying out his mission as God's instrument of judgment on the house of Ahab, and he did destroy Baal worship in Israel (vv.28,30).

However, Jehu stopped right there. He did not go on to re-establish worship of God throughout the land. Instead, he persisted in 'the sins of Jeroboam' (v.29), by allowing worship of the golden calves at Bethel and Dan to continue, probably for the very same reasons Jeroboam had established this corrupt worship of God in the first place (see Chapter 17). Jehu himself participated in this, and failed to follow the ways of the Lord with all his heart, and for this he was condemned (v.31). All Jehu did was to exchange one form of idolatry for another, instead of taking the opportunity he had been given to serve the God who had placed him on the throne of Israel. Like Jehu, do we pay lip service to God while our heart is far from Him?

The fact that, on balance, God disapproved of both the means by which Jehu achieved his mission, and his subsequent actions, is shown in two ways: his dynasty was only allowed to last four more generations (v.30), and during Jehu's reign, the size of Israel's territory diminished, with Hazael, king of Syria, capturing all the land to the east of the River Jordan (vv.32–33).

In spite of what he achieved, Jehu stands condemned for only obeying God when it suited him, rather than submitting himself completely to the service of God. Does our obedience to God depend on what He asks us to do, or are our lives examples of true servanthood?

Chapter 22

Little Boy Lost

Joash

2 Chronicles 22:10–24:27
(2 Kings 11–12)
(Other bit part players appearing: Athaliah, Jehosheba,
Jehoiada, Zechariah)

Smuggled out

Athaliah, the daughter of Ahab and Jezebel, had been married
to Jehoram during the reign of his father, Jehoshaphat, king of
Judah (see Chapter 19). Jehoram had duly succeeded his father as
king of Judah, and reigned for eight years, to be followed on the
throne by Ahaziah, the son of Jehoram and Athaliah. But Ahaziah
reigned for only one year before being put to death by Jehu and
his men (see Chapter 21).

On hearing of the death of her son Ahaziah, Athaliah seized the
throne of Judah, even though she was of the house of Ahab, not
David. Athaliah then 'proceeded to destroy the whole royal family
of the house of Judah' (22:10), which would have the effect of
eliminating the house of David. She was so determined to retain

the power that she had enjoyed firstly as queen, and then as queen mother, that she ruthlessly and callously killed all the royal family – or so she thought. However, one descendant of David managed to survive her purge: her grandson, Joash, a son of Ahaziah. Interestingly, David's line would be saved from extinction, not by God's direct intervention, but by human loyalty and courage.

Joash was hidden from his grandmother, Athaliah, by his aunt, Jehosheba, the sister of Ahaziah (vv.11–12). Jehosheba initially concealed Joash and his nurse in one of the palace bedrooms while Athaliah went on her killing spree. Clearly, Joash couldn't stay there for long undetected, so Jehosheba desperately needed to find another hiding place for her one-year-old nephew. She was married to Jehoiada, the priest, so Jehosheba decided to smuggle Joash and his nurse out of the palace and into the Temple, where they could be hidden far more easily and safely. In the event, Joash remained in hiding for six years while Athaliah ruled the kingdom of Judah.

Counter-coup

In the seventh year of Athaliah's rule, Jehoiada finally plucked up enough courage to take action against the idolatrous queen (23:1–11). The action he was intent on taking could have cost him his life, but Jehoiada knew it was the right thing to do. When faced with the cost of doing what is right in God's sight, are we prepared to take courageous action, or do we prefer to keep quiet and settle for the status quo?

Jehoiada gathered together various disaffected commanders and groups of mercenaries, along with the Levites and heads of families from throughout Judah. There at the Temple they made a covenant together before God to restore the throne to the king's son and legitimate heir, Joash, now aged seven. Jehoiada then outlined detailed and meticulous plans to accomplish their agreed objective. When all was ready and everyone was in place, Joash was proclaimed king, to the jubilation of the people, who flocked to greet him.

Hearing the commotion, Athaliah rushed to the Temple to see what was going on. When she saw Joash standing there as king, and heard all the acclamation, Athaliah tore her robes and screamed 'Treason! Treason!' (v.13) – which was a bit rich coming from her, considering the slaughter she had instigated to seize the throne in the first place! Jehoiada had her put to death by the sword in the palace grounds rather than at the Temple.

Jehoiada then made a covenant with God that 'he and the people and the king would be the LORD's people' (v.16). This affirmed the recommitment of the nation to the covenant made in the time of Moses, which had been largely ignored for more than a century. The first step in cementing this was the removal of all traces of Baal worship which Athaliah had established in Jerusalem. The temple of Baal was demolished, and Mattan, the priest of Baal, was killed. The next step was to restore the worship of God in all its fullness, including all the proper procedures in the Temple as it had been in the time of King David. And so the rightful king was enthroned, and the worship of God was re-established, resulting in rejoicing and peace throughout the kingdom of Judah (vv.16–21).

The Temple repaired

Jehoiada was very much the power behind the throne. As long as Jehoiada was there to advise him, Joash 'did what was right in the eyes of the LORD' (2 Kings 12:2). The Temple buildings had suffered from many years of neglect, so Joash decided that extensive repairs should be undertaken (24:1–14). He instructed the Levites to collect from the people the tax declared by Moses (Exod. 30:11–16) so that these renovations could be funded.

The Levites were rather dilatory about doing this, presumably because they thought the people wouldn't respond willingly. In my experience, those of us in leadership can be guilty sometimes of prejudging how the people will respond, of thinking that a particular project may be a step too far, and therefore of limiting what God can do because of our hesitation. Like the Levites, we can be totally wrong. When Joash made a national proclamation about bringing the tax, the people responded magnificently. All the money was used first to pay the workmen to complete the repairs and the refurbishment, and then the rest was spent on making various articles for use in the Temple.

At a loss

Some years after the work on the Temple was completed, Jehoiada died. Joash actually had him buried with the kings in Jerusalem 'because of the good he had done ... for God and his temple' (v.16). With his trusty advisor gone, Joash seems to have been completely at a loss. He had become so used to relying on Jehoiada since boyhood, that he appears to have found it extremely difficult to make his own decisions. Instead of taking the lead, and building on what had been achieved, Joash turned to his officials. He listened to their advice, and was swayed by their opinions. He even listened to them when their advice took him in a diametrically opposite direction to that advised in the past by Jehoiada (vv.17–22).

Apparently, it never once occurred to Joash to seek God for guidance. Presumably because he became king so young, he had learnt to be dependent on people, and had never matured into putting his personal faith and trust in God. Do we rely totally on other people for advice and guidance? Would we be at a loss without them? Or have we learnt to trust in God for ourselves? Do we always follow the advice people give us, or do we check it out with God's Word first?

The result was disastrous. The transformation that the religious reforms implemented by Joash, under the guidance of Jehoiada, had brought about was completely undermined and sabotaged. 'They abandoned the temple of the LORD, the God of their fathers, and worshipped Asherah poles and idols. Because of their guilt, God's anger came upon Judah and Jerusalem. Although the LORD sent prophets to the people to bring them back to him ... they would not listen' (vv.18–19). On one particular occasion, God's

Spirit came upon Jehoiada's own son, Zechariah, whose message to Joash was blunt and to the point: 'Why do you disobey the LORD's commands? You will not prosper. Because you have forsaken the LORD, he has forsaken you' (v.20).

God in His mercy had graciously sent His prophet to give Joash and the people an opportunity to repent. How do we respond when God faces us up with our sinfulness? Do we seek God's forgiveness, or refuse to listen? Once again, it seems that Joash didn't know what to do. He was persuaded by his officials, all of whom wanted Zechariah silenced, to have the prophet stoned to death. Joash meekly signed the execution order that would result in the death of the son of the man who had advised him for all those years. In a call for justice rather than revenge, Zechariah's dying words to Joash were, 'May the LORD see this and call you to account' (v.22).

Invasion and conspiracy

The following spring, a small Syrian force invaded Judah. The much larger army of Judah was crushed, and all the leaders of the nation were killed. Joash had to resort to bribing Hazael, the king of Syria (Aram), to stop him attacking Jerusalem. Joash sent him 'all the sacred objects ... and the gifts he himself had dedicated and all the gold found in the treasuries of the temple of the LORD and of the royal palace' (2 Kings 12:18). This was seen as judgment on Joash and Judah for forsaking the Lord (v.24).

As a result of this humiliating defeat, the officials whom Joash had trusted and relied upon for advice conspired against him, and assassinated him. What a tragic end to the reign of a man whose early years had promised so much. Interestingly, although Joash was buried in Jerusalem, it seems he was not placed in the tombs of the kings (v.25). Nor is he mentioned in the genealogy of Jesus (Matt. 1:8), one of only three kings not to be included there.

Joash was not practised in the art of making his own decisions. Do we as parents help to equip our own children with these skills by allowing them the freedom to make their own decisions, even if they are bad ones? And when they make wrong decisions, as they surely will, do we help them to learn how to use their experiences to develop the ability to make good decisions in the future? May God give us all the wisdom we need in this critical area of our children's development.

Chapter 23

Half-hearted

Amaziah

2 Chronicles 25
(2 Kings 14:1–21)
(Other bit part player appearing: Jehoash)

The mercenaries

Amaziah was twenty-five years old when he became king following the assassination of his father, Joash (see Chapter 22). From the start of his reign 'He did what was right in the eyes of the LORD, but not wholeheartedly' (25:2). It seems that Amaziah knew what God required of him, but he obeyed the Lord only grudgingly, and probably with a certain amount of resentment. Although Amaziah never ever consulted God about anything, God was gracious and sent prophets to warn him about his actions on two occasions.

Amaziah certainly obeyed the Law of Moses when he avenged his father's assassination by only putting the conspirators to death, and not their sons as well (vv.3–4). He also obeyed God's voice over the matter of the mercenaries, even though it cost him financially to do so (vv.9–10). This situation arose when Amaziah decided to go to war against Edom. He seems to have reached the conclusion that the 300,000 troops available to him would not be sufficient to secure victory, so he increased the size of his army to 400,000 by hiring 100,000 mercenaries from Israel (v.6). When a prophet came and told Amaziah that this was a bad move because God was not with Israel, and if he went into battle with these mercenaries from Israel in his ranks, 'God will overthrow you before the enemy' (v.8), the king sent the hired soldiers home.

This act of obedience, although carried out under protest, resulted in Amaziah winning a great victory (vv.11–12). As the prophet said to Amaziah when he complained about the financial loss he would incur, 'The LORD can give you much more than that' (v.9). This serves to remind us that, when we obey God, He will bless us abundantly (Mal. 3:10; 1 John 3:21–22). Do we ever allow financial considerations to influence our obedience to God? When money talks and God talks, which talks the louder (Matt. 6:24)?

Amaziah never seemed to make the connection between obeying God and being successful. His love for God was at best half-hearted, and he only followed God's ways because he felt he had to. Has our love for God become lukewarm when once it was on fire (Rev. 2:4; 3:16)? Do we obey God grudgingly, and only because we think we've got to; or do we serve Him willingly and wholeheartedly, because we want to (Psa. 119:34; Eph. 6:7)?

The slippery slope

What Amaziah did next clearly illustrates that half-heartedness in serving God, if allowed to persist in our lives, will ultimately result in us going down the slippery slope that leads to us turning our backs on Him and going our own way. Having conquered Edom and Seir, Amaziah inexplicably decided to bring back their gods and worship them, instead of praising the God who had given him the victory. And when he was faced up with this by God's prophet, who asked Amaziah, not unreasonably 'Why do you consult this people's gods, which could not save their own people from your hand?' (v.15), the king promptly told him to shut up, or else! The prophet's parting shot was ominous: 'I know that God has determined to destroy you, because you have done this and have not listened to my counsel' (v.16).

Amaziah's rejection of God was complete, and ultimately led to his downfall. While Amaziah basked in the glory of his recent victory, and must have thought he was on the way up, he was in fact on the slippery slope down to destruction. He had become proud and arrogant, attributing his victory to his own strength, considering himself self-sufficient, and having no need of God any more.

The thistle and the cedar

While Amaziah had been fighting the Edomites, the 100,000 mercenaries from Israel had been exacting their revenge on him. Angered by Amaziah's decision to dismiss them, which cost them the opportunity to benefit from all the plunder available after a victory, the mercenaries had raided several towns in Judah. They had killed 3,000 people, and made off with huge amounts of plunder (v.13).

Amaziah, having sent God's prophet packing, sought the advice of his officials (v.17). Sensing Amaziah's supremely confident mood following his victory, they agreed with his apparent determination to go to war with Israel, which had no doubt been sparked by the actions of the mercenaries. Accordingly, a challenge was sent to Jehoash, the king of Israel.

Jehoash must have known that his army could defeat Judah but, rather than accept the challenge, he tried to avert a conflict. His reply must have come as something of a surprise to Amaziah (vv.18–19). It was in the form of a story about a thistle and a cedar tree: the former clearly representing Judah, and the latter Israel. The thistle was trampled underfoot by a wild beast. Just in case Amaziah hadn't got the message, Jehoash spelt it out: 'You say to yourself that you have defeated Edom, and now you are arrogant and proud. But stay at home! Why ask for trouble and cause your own downfall and that of Judah also?' (v.19).

Blind and deaf

Amaziah, blinded by ambition, and deaf to any voice that contradicted him, prepared for war (vv.20–24). The battle took place at Beth Shemesh in Judah, and Amaziah's army was routed. Amaziah himself was captured, and taken back to Jerusalem in disgrace by Jehoash. The king of Israel then proceeded to destroy part of Jerusalem's defensive wall, and plunder the Temple and palace of their remaining treasures. Jehoash then returned home to Samaria, taking hostages with him. The hand of God was seen to be behind all these events, which were attributed to Amaziah abandoning God and worshipping the idols of Edom (v.20). The words of the prophet had been fulfilled (v.16).

Surprisingly perhaps after such a debacle, Amaziah continued to reign for at least another fifteen years (v.25). He must have known that he had upset many people by abandoning worship of God and embarking on the foolhardy war against Israel. Indeed, it seems conspirators had been plotting against him since he began his idol worship (v.27). We are not told what brought matters to a head, but suddenly, Amaziah fled to Lachish. This was all in vain, because he was pursued and assassinated, like his father before him. Amaziah's body was brought back to Jerusalem for burial (vv.27–28), and his son, Uzziah, became king.

Amaziah's half-heartedness had ended in tragedy. No wonder Jesus was so outspoken about the lukewarmness of the church at Laodicea (Rev. 3:14–20). He desperately wanted them to repent of their half-heartedness before it was too late. It is in this context, and not that of salvation, that we find this well-known verse: 'Here I am! I stand at the door and knock. If anyone hears my voice and opens the door, I will come in and eat with him, and he with me' (Rev. 3:20).

Have we, like the members of the church in Laodicea, become

blind to our half-heartedness, and deaf to Jesus lovingly calling us by name and knocking at the door of our hearts? If so, may God graciously open our eyes and our ears, and give us the courage to respond by opening the door, so that our relationship with Him might be fully restored to what it once was. As Holman Hunt's famous painting of this scene shows, the only handle is on our side of the door.

Chapter 24

Spectacular Transformation

Manasseh

2 Chronicles 33
(2 Kings 21:1–18)
(Other bit part players appearing: Hezekiah, Amon)

Background and heritage

By the time Manasseh came to the throne of Judah at the age of twelve, the northern kingdom of Israel had long since ceased to exist. It had been swallowed up, along with Syria, into the rapidly expanding empire of Assyria to the north. Indeed, Judah itself was attacked by the Assyrians and Jerusalem put under siege during the reign of Manasseh's father, Hezekiah (see 2 Chron. 32). Had God not miraculously intervened, Judah would probably have disappeared as a nation as well. As it was, Judah remained intact, as long as it kept the Assyrians happy. During the reign of Manasseh, another power began to rise in the east to challenge the dominance of Assyria. That power was Babylon.

During his reign, Hezekiah had brought about widespread civil and religious reforms. He had demonstrated a close relationship with God, destroying all vestiges of pagan worship that had crept into the land, and showing himself to be a man of prayer. The Temple had been reopened, renovated and become the centre of worship once again; the Passover feast was being properly observed; the Philistines had been defeated and the Assyrians miraculously repelled; there had even been something of a revival in the religious life of the nation. Indeed, Hezekiah was given as glowing a testimonial as any king could hope for (2 Kings 18:3–8). He was simply the best king of Judah ever.

Detestable practices

Although Manasseh had grown up seeing all this, he set about reversing everything that his father had done. Following the example of his grandfather, Ahaz, he committed many grievous and dreadful sins in the eyes of God (33:3–9). Manasseh desecrated the Temple by building altars to numerous pagan deities there, and worshipping them. These included the gods of the stars worshipped by the Assyrians, along with their other cults, presumably in an attempt to ingratiate himself with them, and establish his own position as their ally. He encouraged various occult practices, including sorcery, divination and witchcraft; he himself consulted mediums and spiritists. But surely the most detestable sin of all that Manasseh committed was the offering of his sons as human sacrifices.

God sent prophets to warn the people of the consequences of following Manasseh's ways. Echoing the words of the prophet Amos to the northern kingdom (also known also as Samaria) many years previously, the prophets told them that God said: 'I am going to bring such disaster on Jerusalem and Judah that the ears of everyone who hears of it will tingle. I will stretch out over Jerusalem the measuring line used against Samaria and the plumb-line used against the house of Ahab. I will wipe out Jerusalem as one wipes out a dish, wiping it and turning it upside-down'

(2 Kings 21:12–13). And plenty more besides! But nobody paid the slightest attention to their warnings.

Turning point

When Manasseh had been on the throne for about forty-five years, the Babylonians decided to flex their muscles, and they rebelled against Assyria. The rebellion was soon put down, but it seems that the Assyrians suspected Manasseh of siding with the Babylonians in their uprising. He was seized, and was humiliated by having a hook put in his nose and being shackled (v.11). Then he was transported to Babylon for trial with the rest of the rebels. This was seen as God's judgment on Manasseh and the people of Judah for paying no heed to the prophets.

This humiliating experience was to prove a turning point in the life of Manasseh. There, in a Babylonian dungeon, something remarkable happened: 'In his distress he sought the favour of the LORD his God and humbled himself greatly before the God of his fathers' (v.12). Manasseh, one of the most evil kings in the history of the kingdom of Judah, got down on his knees, prayed, and asked for God's forgiveness.

How would God respond to the confession of this king, who had been guilty of perpetrating such evil in the eyes of the Lord? 'And when he prayed to him, the LORD was moved by his entreaty and listened to his plea; so he brought him back to Jerusalem and to his kingdom' (v.13). Not only did God forgive him, but he intervened in Manasseh's situation and brought him back to Judah to continue his reign! What an encouragement and cause for rejoicing this wonderful example of God's mercy and grace is for us all. If God is willing to forgive the likes of Manasseh, then we can rest assured that none of us is outside the scope of God's love and forgiveness, no matter what we may have done (Rom. 3:23–24).

Manasseh turned to God when he was in a desperate situation. In my experience, it is often when people reach a crisis point in their lives that they begin to think about God, and come to acknowledge their need of Him. May this encourage us never to give up praying for those whom we know and love, who at this moment are far away from God. Who knows what tomorrow may bring? It may just prove to be a turning point in their lives.

Restoration

How do we know that Manasseh's repentance was real, and not just a desperate charade to get him out of the mess he was in? The proof that this spectacular transformation was undoubtedly genuine can be seen in the actions Manasseh took during the rest of his reign (vv.15–16). He got rid of all images and altars to pagan gods both inside the Temple and in the city of Jerusalem, which ran the risk of angering the Assyrians; he restored the worship of God and sacrifices to the Lord at the altar in the Temple, and he commanded the people to serve the Lord.

However, in spite of Manasseh's efforts, this attempt at restoring the worship of God didn't really take root within the kingdom. When Manasseh died, his son Amon succeeded him. Amon simply swept aside the changes his father had made, and restored the pagan worship Manasseh had originally established in the kingdom (v.22). This would have had the added effect of signalling to the all-powerful Assyrians that he wasn't a potential renegade like his father. But after reigning for only two years, Amon would be assassinated, and replaced by his eight-year-old son, Josiah (vv.24–25).

Chapter 25

Godly and Obedient

Josiah

2 Chronicles 34–35
(2 Kings 22:1–23:30)

(Other bit part players appearing: Hilkiah, Huldah, Nebuchadnezzar,
Neco, Jehoiakim, Jehoiachin, Zedekiah)

Impact for God

Josiah, like Joash before him (see Chapter 22), came to the throne at
a very young age (34:1), and grew up to institute various religious
reforms which would bring the people of Judah back to the worship
of God. Josiah's accession to the throne at the age of eight was not
as dramatic as that of Joash; it followed the assassination of his
father Amon at the hands of a group of disgruntled conspirators,
who themselves were put to death by others (33:24–25). Josiah
would be king of Judah for thirty-one years (v.1).

When he was sixteen, Josiah seems to have made a real
commitment to serve God, and began to 'seek the God of his
father David' (v.3) for wisdom and guidance in his life. Four years

later, at the age of twenty, Josiah's personal commitment began to impact the kingdom, as he ordered and directed the destruction of all vestiges of pagan worship that had permeated the land during the reigns of his father Amon and grandfather Manasseh (vv.3–7). This purge would be carried out more fully and thoroughly after the discovery of the Book of the Law in the Temple six years later.

Interestingly, a year after the young Josiah had begun his purge, Jeremiah was called by God to be a prophet. He was very reluctant to accept this calling in view of his youthfulness, but God assured Jeremiah that age didn't matter, and that he would give him the words to speak (Jer. 1:2,6–10). So here we have two young men, dedicated to the service of God, ministering in Judah at the same time – and both would have a massive impact on the nation.

Do we encourage and nurture the ministry of the young people in our churches, or do we look down on it and belittle it? Yes, they will make mistakes due to lack of spiritual experience, but isn't it better to guide them and help them to develop spiritually than to criticise them unfairly and curtail their activities? No one is too young to serve God, provided they are teachable, their lives are in keeping with what they profess to believe, they show a degree of spiritual maturity, and they seek advice before doing anything. But then, isn't that true for all of us? And who knows the impact for God that those young people will grow up to have in our nation if we nurture them properly?

The Book of the Law

In the eighteenth year of his reign, Josiah instigated a programme of building works to repair and restore the Temple in Jerusalem to something like its former glory (vv.8–13). At some point during this period of restoration, Hilkiah the high priest found 'the Book of the Law of the LORD that had been given through Moses' (v.14). This could well have been the book of Deuteronomy, which had seemingly been lost during the period of the evil kings of Judah.

Hilkiah sent Shaphan, the secretary, to Josiah with the Book of the Law, and Shaphan began to read it to the king. Josiah was shaken to the core by what he heard, and realised that what he had implemented so far had but scratched the surface of what God required of His people. Josiah tore his robes in grief and wept in sorrow at the failure of himself and the people to live holy lives before God as set out in the Book. Josiah's conclusion was: 'Great is the LORD's anger that is poured out on us because our fathers have not kept the word of the LORD; they have not acted in accordance with all that is written in this book' (v.21). Do we live our lives in accordance with the teachings of the Bible? As we read God's Word and hear it preached do we, like Josiah, obey its teaching and change our ways?

Josiah realised that he needed to seek the Lord about this matter, so he asked a group led by Hilkiah to 'enquire of the LORD' (v.21) on his behalf. They in turn consulted a prophetess named Huldah, through whom God declared that the sins of the people down the years were going to result in God's anger being visited upon Judah, with disastrous consequences for the nation. But because Josiah had responded in the way he had, God's judgment would not fall during his reign, which would be characterised by peace (vv.22–28). Josiah would be spared seeing the fall of Judah and Jerusalem, which took place within sixty years of his death.

The purge continued

Hearing the contents of the Book of the Law spurred Josiah on in his campaign to purge the land of everything that smacked of pagan worship. In so doing, Josiah was following in the footsteps of his great-grandfather, Hezekiah (see Chapter 24), who had brought the nation back to worship God, although Josiah's purge was even more extensive and far-reaching. It even included the demolishing and defiling of the high place at Bethel set up by Jeroboam (see Chapter 17), thereby fulfilling the prophecy concerning it (1 Kings 13:1–2; 2 Kings 23:15–18).

Josiah was also defying the Assyrians by banishing worship of their gods not only from Judah, but also from parts of the old kingdom of Israel, now under Assyrian control. Even though Assyria had greater problems to worry about at the time than the defiance of a relatively unimportant vassal, it was still a courageous move on the part of Josiah, and showed that he was dead set on restoring the worship of God, whatever the cost.

Josiah proceeded to renew the covenant in the Temple, and insisted that the people pledged themselves to serving God once again (vv.31–32). This was followed by the ark being restored to its proper place, and a magnificent celebration of the Passover, unparalleled since the time of Samuel (35:3,18). Unfortunately, as thorough as Josiah's measures and reforms were, they never really touched the hearts and minds of the people, who went along with the king more out of respect for him rather than because they shared his convictions. This is reflected in the prophecies of Jeremiah at that time (Jer. 2–6).

The battle of Megiddo

In the twenty-eighth year of Josiah's reign, the Babylonians led by Nebuchadnezzar captured the Assyrian capital, Nineveh. Three years later, the Babylonians moved in force to finish off the Assyrians, who had regrouped at Carchemish. Neco, the Pharaoh of Egypt, marched his army north in support of the Assyrians. This meant him passing through Judah, which Josiah regarded as a threat to his kingdom, despite strong reassurances from Neco to the contrary. Neco even claimed that God had sent him on this mission (vv.20–21).

Surprisingly, in view of what we know about Josiah, he did not consult God on the matter, but rather went out in disguise to do battle with Neco. Perhaps Josiah feared that if Neco and the Assyrians defeated Babylon, they would turn on Judah and divide it up between them. Whatever his reason, battle was joined at Megiddo, and Josiah was killed during the fighting (vv.22–24). Neco went on to join the Assyrians, but the Babylonians were victorious, and became the dominant power in the region. Josiah was buried in Jerusalem, and Jeremiah composed laments for him (v.25).

While his great-grandfather Hezekiah was remembered for his faith in God, Josiah was remembered for his obedience to God and His laws. Josiah was always prepared to acknowledge sin, to deal with sin, and to remove the causes of sin. Are we prepared to adopt a similar process in our lives, including taking steps to avoid reading certain literature, watching certain programmes, going to certain places, and being near certain people, in order to remove the possibility of temptation (Matt. 5:29–30)?

The end of Judah

After Josiah's death, the kingdom of Judah became a vassal of Egypt. His son, Jehoahaz, reigned for only three months before the Egyptians replaced him with Jehoiakim, another of Josiah's sons. During Jehoiakim's reign, Nebuchadnezzar's Babylonian army defeated the Egyptians under Neco, and took over all their vassal states, including Judah.

When Jehoiakim rashly decided to rebel against Babylon, Nebuchadnezzar sent local Babylonian garrison troops into Judah. Jehoiakim was captured, and died shortly afterwards. He was succeeded by his son, Jehoiachin. When the main Babylonian force finally arrived in Judah, they looted the Temple and took most of the leaders of Judah back to Babylon as prisoners, including Jehoiachin. Nebuchadnezzar replaced him as king with another son of Josiah named Zedekiah. When he also rebelled nine years later, the Babylonians returned. After a siege lasting over eighteen months, the Babylonians finally destroyed Jerusalem, including the Temple, in 586 BC. The disaster Huldah had prophesied had come to pass.

The Babylonian policy was to take only the leaders of a nation, along with the strongest and most skilled men, off to Babylon. There they were allowed to live and work together. This enabled the Jews to remain united and faithful to God during their seventy years in Exile, and paved the way for their return to Jerusalem, firstly under the leadership of Zerubbabel (see Chapter 27), then Ezra the priest, and finally Nehemiah.

Chapter 26

No Compromise

Shadrach, Meshach and Abednego

Daniel 3
(Other bit part player appearing: Nebuchadnezzar)

New names

Following the destruction of the kingdom of Judah and its capital city Jerusalem by the forces of King Nebuchadnezzar, the royal family and nobility of Judah were carried off into exile in Babylon. Daniel and his friends Hananiah, Mishael and Azariah were among those chosen from the noble families of Judah to be sent on a three-year academic training course, during which they would be re-educated in the ways and culture of Babylon, ready to take up positions in the king's service.

The Babylonians were trying to change both their thinking and their beliefs. They wanted to re-program them both mentally and spiritually. As part of this process, they gave the four of them new Babylonian names. Daniel, whose name means 'God is my judge', was given the name Belteshazzar, meaning 'Bel, protect his life'. Bel, or Marduk, was the chief god of the Babylonians. Hananiah, which means 'the Lord shows grace', was renamed

Shadrach, meaning 'under the command of Aku', the moon god. Mishael, meaning 'who is like God?' was given the name Meshach, meaning 'who is like Aku?'. Azariah, which means 'the Lord helps' was renamed Abednego, meaning 'servant of Nego', another name for Nabu, the god of learning and writing.

In those days, a person's name was very important. It spoke of your whole identity. Changing their names was all part of the pressure being applied to these young men to assimilate themselves into the culture of Babylon, to conform to its ways, and to transfer their allegiance from the God of Israel to the gods of Babylon; to forget that they were Jews, and become Babylonians in every respect.

Excellence in adversity

These four young men proved to be excellent students, and when they were interviewed by Nebuchadnezzar at the end of their training, 'he found none equal to Daniel, Hananiah, Mishael and Azariah; so they entered the king's service. In every matter of wisdom and understanding about which the king questioned them, he found them ten times better than all the magicians and enchanters in his whole kingdom' (1:19–20). Although they had been subjected to this programme of brainwashing, Daniel and his friends had remained steadfastly loyal to their God, who had given them a 'wisdom and understanding' that allowed them an insight which the Babylonian advisors did not have.

However distasteful this training may have been to them, these young men undoubtedly saw God's leading in all this. They must have talked and prayed together about it a great deal. They clearly believed that God had a purpose, and were prepared to trust Him. In the end, they finished up as three of Nebuchadnezzar's most sought-after advisors. Along with Daniel, they were God's men in Babylon, and would go on to have a great impact on Nebuchadnezzar and his kingdom.

How do we react when we find ourselves in situations we

would rather not be in? Do we still do our best and seek to honour God in them, believing that God is working out His purposes in our lives, even though we may not see how? Do we see ourselves as God's man or woman in that situation, and look to influence matters for the better? Paul tells us that in whatever situation we find ourselves we are 'Christ's ambassadors' (2 Cor. 5:20), and should act accordingly, just as Daniel and his friends did.

The way that society is nowadays in much of the western world can make us feel that we too, as Christians, are living in a foreign culture. The prevailing attitudes and mores that bombard us in the media, the gods of materialism and hedonism that are worshipped everywhere, and all the other things that go on are as distasteful to us as the Babylonian culture was to Daniel and his friends. The pressure to conform is enormous, particularly among our young people. How much we all need God's strength and courage to stand up and be counted, and to seek to impact our society and influence what is happening! How we need to pray, not only for ourselves, but also for our brothers and sisters in those many countries of the world where the persecution of Christians is rife, that our faith may not fail, and that we may truly be ambassadors for Christ.

Bow or burn

Like many emperors before and after him, Nebuchadnezzar sought to unite and cement together the many disparate nations, tribes and cultures he ruled over by creating something they could all have in common: a particular act of worship, which would strengthen the power of the emperor and his hold over the citizens of his empire. In the Roman Empire it was worship of the emperor himself; in the Babylonian Empire it was worship of an image of gold set up by the emperor.

This towering golden pillar was almost one hundred feet high and ten feet wide (v.1), and could be seen for miles around. It was tantamount to a symbol of the power of Nebuchadnezzar. At a packed dedication ceremony out there on the plain of Dura, a herald proclaimed in a very loud voice what Nebuchadnezzar had decreed in his script concerning this image of gold: 'O peoples, nations and men of every language: As soon as you hear the sound of the horn, flute, zither, lyre, harp, pipes and all kinds of music, you must fall down and worship the image of gold that King Nebuchadnezzar has set up. Whoever does not fall down and worship will immediately be thrown into a blazing furnace' (vv.4–6). It was a case of either bow or burn!

Not surprisingly, everyone was flat on their faces as fast as they could get there whenever the music played (v.7)! Well, almost everyone, that is. It didn't take some of Nebuchadnezzar's advisors long to realise that certain young men at the court were not putting their noses to the ground as commanded (v.8). Interestingly, for some reason Daniel was not on their list – perhaps he was away on the king's business in a far-flung province at the time – but Shadrach, Meshach and Abednego certainly were (v.12).

Motives

These whistle-blowing advisors were undoubtedly motivated by jealousy and prejudice as well as indignation at the effrontery of these three Jews in disobeying the king's decree concerning the golden image. Here they saw a golden opportunity to get rid of these Jews, whose wisdom and advice the king always seemed to prefer to theirs. They didn't bother to investigate whether other Jews were similarly guilty: Shadrach, Meshach and Abednego were the ones they wanted eliminated.

Do we ever act out of jealousy or prejudice towards people? Do we sometimes dress these emotions up as something else – such as indignation perhaps – or act under some pretext or other that hides our true motives? Paul warns us to get rid of such destructive emotions as jealousy and hatred, which have no place in the kingdom of God, and that one day the true motives of our hearts will be exposed (Gal. 5:20; 1 Cor. 4:5).

Obedience

When he heard the accusations of his advisors, Nebuchadnezzar, never a man noted for his moderation, went ballistic, and summoned Shadrach, Meshach and Abednego to appear before him at once, if not sooner (v.13). This egocentric tyrant wasn't used to being disobeyed, even when his demands were unreasonable. Nebuchadnezzar's viewpoint would doubtless have been that these three Jewish non-conformists were undermining his authority, and that such instances of disobedience could not be tolerated if he was to maintain his grip of absolute power on the empire.

Nebuchadnezzar must have been shocked that three of his most trusted and important advisors were defying him in this way; so instead of condemning them to the flames immediately, he was prepared to give them a second chance (vv.14–15). But Shadrach, Meshach and Abednego were not prepared to compromise.

When this golden image was first set up, the three friends must have discussed together what they were going to do. Perhaps they rehearsed many of the arguments that we all do when we are tempted to make compromises in our lifestyle, such as, it's only a small thing, so it doesn't really matter; we'll just pretend to go along with it, but we won't mean it deep down; God understands the pressure we're under, so He won't mind; God is merciful, so He will forgive us for doing it; everybody else is doing it, and we don't want to appear strange.

These may sound plausible, but they represent flawed reasoning. When we compromise with the world, are we not in fact disobeying God (1 Pet. 1:14)? Shadrach, Meshach and Abednego knew this to be true. To obey the king meant to disobey God: they would be breaking the second commandment (Exod. 20:3). Compromise was never a possibility for them, even though they knew they would inevitably be caught and burned alive. For Shadrach, Meshach and Abednego, obedience to God was more important than their own lives. Now there's a challenge for each one of us!

The problem with compromise is, where does it stop? In my experience, compromise is like a cancer that starts small, but then eats its way through the whole of our lifestyle, and destroys our credibility and witness as Christ's ambassadors. No wonder Paul exhorts us: 'Do not conform any longer to the pattern of this world, but be transformed by the renewing of your mind' (Rom. 12:2). Is our allegiance to God, or to the world?

Faith at the furnace

However much they may have prepared themselves for this moment, when it actually came Shadrach, Meshach and Abednego must have felt under immense pressure to make that little compromise to avoid the flames of the furnace. But they didn't. They were totally resolute in their obedience to God. As they stood there before Nebuchadnezzar, they made this amazing statement of faith: 'If we are thrown into the blazing furnace, the God we serve is able to save us from it, and he will rescue us from your hand, O king' (v.17). Even when faced with the flames of the furnace, they held fast to their faith and trust in God. How do we fare when our faith is severely tested? In my experience, it's not easy to stand firm in such situations, but God will give us the grace, strength and courage to do so, if we hold on to Him (Isa. 41:13).

In his arrogance, Nebuchadnezzar had challenged Shadrach, Meshach and Abednego with the words, 'what god will be able to rescue you from my hand?' (v.15). Their reply told him in no uncertain terms that there was indeed a God who could save them. They bravely voiced their unquestioning belief that their God was able – able to do anything; even to miraculously rescue them from the flames. When we pray, do we show that kind of faith, believing with all our heart that the God we serve is able to do absolutely anything; that nothing is impossible for Him to do (Luke 1:37; 17:6)?

But their statement of faith didn't end there. They continued boldly: 'But even if he does not, we want you to know, O king, that we will not serve your gods or worship the image of gold you have set up' (v.18). Shadrach, Meshach and Abednego were prepared to face the flames rather than to compromise. Their love for and obedience to God did not depend on whether or not He answered their prayers, or did something miraculous for them. They loved and obeyed Him simply because He was worthy. Do we love God in the same unconditional and selfless way? Do we obey God because we love Him, and not because of what He might do for us in return? What does our love for God depend on?

God could have intervened and rescued them. He could have stopped them from going into the furnace; He could have slain Nebuchadnezzar there and then; He could have sent His angels to sort out the guards and soldiers – but He did none of these things. Instead, He allowed His faithful, obedient servants to be thrown into the fiery furnace.

It seems to me that there is a very important lesson for us to learn here: we must be prepared for the fact that God may not bring us out of the trial that we are going through. Shadrach, Meshach and Abednego had faced up to that possibility, and had come to terms with it, and so must we. They did not allow it to affect their love, obedience and determination not to give in. Will we?

Fury at the furnace

Predictably, Nebuchadnezzar was absolutely furious, and his attitude towards Shadrach, Meshach and Abednego changed dramatically for the worse (vv.19–21). He screamed that the furnace should be heated seven times hotter than it usually was. He ordered his strongest soldiers to tie up Shadrach, Meshach and Abednego as tightly as possible, and throw them into the furnace.

The 'blazing furnace' (v.20) would have been very large, similar in size to those used in industry for brickmaking or smelting metal. The fearsome flames would have leapt into the air above the top of the furnace; in fact, they killed the soldiers who threw Shadrach, Meshach and Abednego in (v.22). Nebuchadnezzar was obviously watching proceedings from a discreet distance, because no sooner had he seen Shadrach, Meshach and Abednego falling through the flames into the furnace than he was on his feet, gasping in amazement.

The fourth man

Nebuchadnezzar turned to his advisors, and asked, 'Weren't there three men that we tied up and threw into the fire?' (v.24). Were they the same group who had shopped Shadrach, Meshach and Abednego in the first place, and had come to see the fun? If so, then they were in for a bit of a shock! 'Certainly, O king', they replied (v.24), somewhat bewildered. Nebuchadnezzar's face must have been an absolute picture as he no doubt pointed towards the furnace, his arm shaking in fear, and his voice shrieking and trembling and gasping in disbelief as he said, 'Look! I see four men walking around in the fire, unbound and unharmed, and the fourth looks like a son of the gods' (v.25).

What a wonderful picture this portrays of the truth that, whatever trials we go through in life, we are never alone. God is always right there with us in our trials, walking with us, talking with us, comforting us, encouraging us. Was this fourth man Jesus Himself? Was it an angel of the Lord? Whoever it was, God was present with them in that fiery furnace.

Shadrach, Meshach and Abednego's obedience to God and their uncompromising stand was totally vindicated. When they emerged from the furnace at Nebuchadnezzar's behest, it was observed by all that 'the fire had not harmed their bodies, nor was a hair of their heads singed; their robes were not scorched, and there was no smell of fire on them' (v.27). How amazing is that! Nebuchadnezzar was suitably impressed. He publicly praised the God of Shadrach, Meshach and Abednego, and rewarded the three of them by promoting them to higher office (vv.28–30).

Imagine the tremendous effect that this incident would have had on the faith of all the Jews there in exile in Babylon. And did Isaiah anticipate this incident when he wrote: 'When you walk through the fire, you will not be burned; the flames will not set you ablaze. For I am the LORD, your God, the Holy One of Israel, your Saviour' (Isa. 43:2–3)?

Chapter 27

By My Spirit

Zerubbabel

Ezra 1:1–5:2
(Other bit part players appearing: Jeshua, Haggai, Zechariah)

Return to Jerusalem

In 539 BC, forty-seven years after the Babylonians destroyed Jerusalem under Nebuchadnezzar, the Persians conquered Babylon, and took over as the dominant power in the region. Their foreign policy was to allow captured peoples to return home. King Cyrus of Persia, who was rather more merciful to conquered nations than previous emperors of Assyria and Babylon had been, reasoned that such action would produce loyalty and willing allegiance to him on the part of those subjugated countries.

Under this policy, the Jews were allowed to return to Jerusalem and begin work on rebuilding the Temple the following year. Cyrus issued a decree to this effect, and also generously returned all the 5,400 articles of gold and silver which Nebuchadnezzar had stolen from the Temple in Jerusalem (1:7–11). Zerubbabel brought these precious items back with him when he returned to Judah. About 50,000 Jews made the journey back to Jerusalem under his leadership in 538 BC. More would follow in subsequent years, under the leadership of Ezra in 458 BC, and Nehemiah in 445 BC.

Zerubbabel was the grandson of Jehoiachin, the penultimate king of Judah before the destruction of the Temple (see Chapter 25), so he was a descendant of King David, and an ancestor of Jesus (Matt. 1:12–13). But, more importantly, the people recognised that Zerubbabel had the necessary leadership qualities, and had willingly accepted him as their governor back in Babylon, a title which they continued to use when referring to him (2:63).

Statement of intent

Where do you begin when faced with a city reduced to rubble? Zerubbabel realised that the most important thing to do was to re-establish the worship of God in Jerusalem. So, after a short time of settling down in their new surroundings, work began on the rebuilding of the Temple on its original site. The heads of each family had already contributed as much as they were able towards this massive project (vv.68–69). Not surprisingly, the money available fell well short of what King David had amassed for the building of the original Temple; in fact, Solomon had 1,000 times as much money at his disposal when he began work as Zerubbabel had (1 Chron. 22:14).

Before starting work laying the foundations for the Temple walls, Zerubbabel, along with Jeshua the priest, his fellow priests and associates 'began to build the altar of the God of Israel to sacrifice burnt offerings on it, in accordance with what is written in the Law of Moses' (3:2). By doing this, they were making a statement that they were totally committed to serving God, would not be drawn into the worship of the foreign gods of their neighbours, and were rededicating themselves to Him to live their lives in accordance with God's laws. This was a bold move, surrounded as they were by peoples who did not welcome their return, and was done 'Despite their fear' that an attack upon them was imminent (v.3).

Are we courageous enough to make such a statement of intent in the place where we find ourselves, even though humanly speaking we may be afraid of what the consequences might be? Significantly, the Jews also celebrated the Feast of Tabernacles (Lev. 23:33–36). This feast reminded them of God's protection and guidance experienced by their forefathers throughout the forty years in the wilderness, and reassured them that God's love for them was just the same. As we make a stand for God in these days when many gods are still worshipped, will we not also experience His love, His protection and His guidance?

Foundations laid

Zerubbabel now turned his attention to the rebuilding of the Temple itself. Wisely, he allowed Jeshua, the priests and the Levites to supervise the work, starting with the laying of the foundations (vv.8–9). Zerubbabel himself would undoubtedly have been the key player in negotiating terms with the Phoenicians to supply the wood for the building of the Temple, as they had done for Solomon (see 2 Chron. 2), as well as making sure the masons and carpenters were paid (v.7).

When the foundations had been laid, a noisy and enthusiastic service of praise, thanksgiving and celebration was held (vv.10–11). There was music, shouting, and much singing, including words from one of David's psalms, 'he is good; his love to Israel endures for ever' (see 1 Chron. 16:34,41). But the shouts of joy were mingled with the sound of much weeping on the part of the older Jews who had seen the original Temple, because they knew that this new Temple was going to be nothing like as glorious and spectacular as the old one (vv.12–13). Did that put a bit of a damper on proceedings for Zerubbabel and his generation?

Are we ever guilty of looking back to the 'good old days',

and regaling the younger generation with how much better and wonderful it was in the Church in those times? Do we ever consider how discouraging that can be, especially since, in my experience, it's often done through glory-tinted spectacles? The question could be asked: 'If it was so wonderful, how come it was lost, and who allowed that to happen?' Isn't it true that looking back is only helpful if it informs and encourages us in our current situation, and gives a springboard and impetus to move on? It seems to me that God continually wants to do new things among His people, and can be hampered by those of us who have eyes only for the past.

Zerubbabel must have got really fed up with hearing about the glories of the old Temple, but did not allow that to deflect him from his God-given task of rebuilding the Temple. He knew that, as interesting as the past might be, he needed to concern himself with the present, accept the situation as it was, and get on with the job of restoring the nation under God's guidance. Isn't that what we should be doing?

Effective tactics

The success of the Jews in getting to this stage only served to raise the hackles of their neighbours, particularly the Samaritans to the north. They were a mixture of foreign peoples drafted in to the old northern kingdom of Israel by the Assyrians when they had conquered it. They had intermarried with the Israelites, and become known as the Samaritans, because the area in which they lived was called Samaria. They saw a rebuilt Temple and city of Jerusalem in a potentially prosperous Jewish state as a threat to their security and economic welfare, and decided to do something about it well before it got to that stage.

The Samaritans employed various clever tactics in an attempt to wipe out this perceived threat. First of all, they sought to infiltrate the Jews in the hope of destroying them from within. They came to Zerubbabel offering to help build the Temple, saying that they worshipped God too (4:1–2). This was a half-truth, because the Samaritans did worship God, but alongside a number of pagan gods. It didn't take Zerubbabel, Jeshua and the family heads long to realise what these Samaritans were up to. They soon sent them away with a flea in their ear, saying, 'You have no part with us in building a temple to our God' (v.3).

Having failed to infiltrate them, the Samaritans then resorted to emotional and psychological warfare. They began a sustained campaign of intimidation and discouragement calculated to wear them down emotionally and play on their fears, which would destroy their will to keep on building (v.4). At the same time, the Samaritans hired counsellors to 'work against them and frustrate their plans' in every way possible, wearing them down psychologically (v.5). This went on unceasingly year after year.

Gradually, these tactics had the desired effect. Zerubbabel himself, along with the people, became so discouraged and fearful that the building project eventually ground to a complete halt after about six years. In my experience, discouragement, fear and infiltration are still three of the most effective tactics used by Satan against the Church today. How important it is for us to encourage one another to keep doing God's work, to maintain our collective faith and trust in God, and to know what His Word says so that false teaching can be rooted out.

Greater glory

After a period of about ten years, during which the people concentrated their energies on building up their own houses rather than God's, two prophets appeared on the scene: Haggai and Zechariah (5:1). Haggai rebuked them for their complacency and lethargy, telling them that it was no wonder they had become dissatisfied with their lot. Their priorities were all wrong (Hag. 1:1–11). They had succumbed to discouragement and neglected God's house, which is why they were not experiencing God's blessing in their lives. They were to put this right immediately, and complete the building of the Temple. As they did so, God would be with them and strengthen them (Hag. 1:13; 2:4).

God's wonderful promise to them was that 'The glory of this present house will be greater than the glory of the former house' (Hag. 2:9). Considering what had happened in Solomon's Temple that was some promise – and some rebuke for those who had bemoaned the fact that this new Temple wouldn't be a patch on the old! This serves as a reminder to us that it's not the building that God looks at; rather He looks at the hearts of the people who are in it.

Not by might

Zechariah also spoke into the situation. He brought a word from God especially for Zerubbabel, and it was this: '"Not by might nor by power, but by my Spirit," says the LORD Almighty. "What are you, O mighty mountain? Before Zerubbabel you will become level ground ... The hands of Zerubbabel have laid the foundation of this temple; his hands will also complete it"' (Zech. 4:6–9).

Zerubbabel was not to trust in his own strength, but in the power of the Spirit of God. Although he and the people felt weak, discouraged and not up to the task, God's power would bring them through to victory. No form of opposition, be it the size of a mountain, would be able to stand against them as they went forward in faith and in the power of the Spirit. God promised Zerubbabel that just as he had started the work, so he would complete it.

What a tremendous confidence boost this must have been to Zerubbabel personally. After all, he bore the ultimate responsibility for the work having stopped, but God was giving him a chance to put the matter right. To their credit, Zerubbabel, Joshua and the people responded magnificently (Hag. 1:12), and as they did so, 'the LORD stirred up the spirit of Zerubbabel ... governor of Judah' (Hag. 1:14), along with the spirit of all the people. Haggai and Zechariah pitched in and helped the workers too (Ezra 5:2). Four years later, in 516 BC, the Temple was completed and dedicated with great joy and jubilation, seventy years after its destruction by the Babylonians (Ezra 6:14–18).

Do we rely on our own strength to accomplish things for God rather than on His Spirit? Do we find it difficult to persist in God's work when faced with opposition and difficulties that assume mountainous proportions? Do we become weary, lose faith, become discouraged and downhearted in our service for God? If we are honest, we all do – and more often than we'd like to admit! But let's be encouraged by what happened to Zerubbabel. Although he failed God in many ways, he learnt to rely on God's strength and to move in the power of God's Spirit – and so can we. This not only applies to us individually, but also collectively as God's people. In our churches, are we open to the moving of the Spirit of God? Do we rely on God, or on our own resources? After all, is it not the Spirit of God who convicts people of sin, and who causes the work we do for Him to bear fruit (1 Thess. 1:5; 1 Cor. 3:6)?

King and priest

Zechariah also had a vision concerning the crowning of Jeshua as high priest (Zech. 6:9–15). Significantly, the name Jeshua is a variant of Joshua, which means 'the Lord saves'. The name Jesus is the Greek equivalent. In this vision, Zechariah saw the distinct and separate roles of king and priest becoming combined in one person. This would be fulfilled in the coming of the Messiah – Jesus, the one who saves. This figure, whom Zechariah referred to as 'the Branch', would be worthy to sit on the throne both as king and priest: 'It is he who will build the temple of the LORD, and he will be clothed with majesty and will sit and rule on his throne. And he will be a priest on his throne. And there will be harmony between the two' (Zech. 6:13).

This was impossible in Jewish thinking. So much so, that some Jews expected there to be two Messiahs – one kingly and the other priestly. But in Jesus, these two offices were to be united: He would be both the King of kings and our great High Priest (Heb. 1,7), as symbolised by the Magi's gifts of gold and frankincense. God would do the 'impossible' to make it possible for each one of us to know Him personally, because He loves us so much. What an encouragement that is to each one of us as we seek to serve Him day by day! In the words of Paul: 'May our Lord Jesus Christ himself and God the Father, who loved us and by his grace gave us eternal encouragement and good hope, encourage your hearts and strengthen you in every good deed and word' (2 Thess. 2:16–17). Amen to that!

Index of Characters

National Distributors

UK: (and countries not listed below)
CWR, Waverley Abbey House, Waverley Lane, Farnham, Surrey GU9 8EP.
Tel: (01252) 784700 Outside UK (44) 1252 784700

AUSTRALIA: CMC Australasia, PO Box 519, Belmont, Victoria 3216.
Tel: (03) 5241 3288 Fax: (03) 5241 3290

CANADA: David C Cook Distribution Canada, PO Box 98, 55 Woodslee Avenue, Paris, Ontario N3L 3E5.
Tel: 1800 263 2664

GHANA: Challenge Enterprises of Ghana, PO Box 5723, Accra.
Tel: (021) 222437/223249 Fax: (021) 226227

HONG KONG: Cross Communications Ltd, 1/F, 562A Nathan Road, Kowloon.
Tel: 2780 1188 Fax: 2770 6229

INDIA: Crystal Communications, 10-3-18/4/1, East Marredpalli, Secunderabad – 500026, Andhra Pradesh. Tel/Fax:
(040) 27737145

KENYA: Keswick Books and Gifts Ltd, PO Box 10242, Nairobi.
Tel: (02) 331692/226047 Fax: (02) 728557

MALAYSIA: Salvation Book Centre (M) Sdn Bhd, 23 Jalan SS 2/64, 47300 Petaling Jaya, Selangor.
Tel: (03) 78766411/78766797 Fax: (03) 78757066/78756360

NEW ZEALAND: CMC Australasia, PO Box 303298, North Harbour, Auckland 0751.
Tel: 0800 449 408 Fax: 0800 449 049

NIGERIA: FBFM, Helen Baugh House, 96 St Finbarr's College Road, Akoka, Lagos.
Tel: (01) 7747429/4700218/825775/827264

PHILIPPINES: OMF Literature Inc, 776 Boni Avenue, Mandaluyong City.
Tel: (02) 531 2183 Fax: (02) 531 1960

SINGAPORE: Alby Commercial Enterprises Pte Ltd, 95 Kallang Avenue #04-00, AIS Industrial Building, 339420. Tel:
(65) 629 27238 Fax: (65) 629 27235

SOUTH AFRICA: Struik Christian Books, 80 MacKenzie Street, PO Box 1144, Cape Town 8000.
Tel: (021) 462 4360 Fax: (021) 461 3612

SRI LANKA: Christombu Publications (Pvt) Ltd, Bartleet House, 65 Braybrooke Place, Colombo 2.
Tel: (9411) 2421073/2447665

TANZANIA: CLC Christian Book Centre, PO Box 1384, Mkwepu Street, Dar es Salaam.
Tel/Fax: (022) 2119439

USA: David C Cook Distribution Canada, PO Box 98, 55 Woodslee Avenue, Paris, Ontario N3L 3E5, Canada.
Tel: 1800 263 2664

ZIMBABWE: Word of Life Books (Pvt) Ltd, Christian Media Centre, 8 Aberdeen Road, Avondale, PO Box A480
Avondale, Harare. Tel: (04) 333355 or 091301188

For email addresses, visit the CWR website: www.cwr.org.uk

CWR is a Registered Charity – Number 294387

CWR is a Limited Company registered in England – Registration Number 1990308

Day and Residential Courses
Counselling Training
Leadership Development
Biblical Study Courses
Regional Seminars
Ministry to Women
Daily Devotionals
Books and Videos
Conference Centre

Trusted all Over the World

CWR HAS GAINED A WORLDWIDE reputation as a centre of excellence for Bible-based training and resources. From our headquarters at Waverley Abbey House, Farnham, England, we have been serving God's people for over 40 years with a vision to help apply God's Word to everyday life and relationships. The daily devotional *Every Day with Jesus* is read by nearly a million readers an issue in more than 150 countries, and our unique courses in biblical studies and pastoral care are respected all over the world. Waverley Abbey House provides a conference centre in a tranquil setting.

For free brochures on our seminars and courses, conference facilities, or a catalogue of CWR resources, please contact us at the following address.
CWR, Waverley Abbey House, Waverley Lane, Farnham, Surrey GU9 8EP, UK

Telephone: +44 (0)1252 784700
Email: mail@cwr.org.uk
Website: www.cwr.org.uk

 Applying God's Word
to everyday life and relationships

Cover to Cover Complete

Taking you on a chronological journey through the Bible, this one-year reading plan allows you to follow the events as they happened – and enables you to see more clearly the unfolding of God's purpose over the centuries. It's also constructed to encourage you to read the entire Bible text in one year.

Based on the original *Cover to Cover Complete: Through the Bible as it happened* with maps, charts, illustrations, diagrams, timelines and notes, but now including the full Bible text, it has everything you need to enhance your understanding as you read. Including the highly-respected Holman Christian Standard Bible (HCSB) text, it also links to a special section on our website, giving access to even more information about key Bible personalities and events.

ISBN: 978-1-85345-433-2
Only £19.99 (plus p&p)

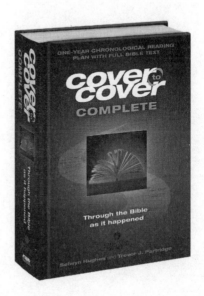

Cover to Cover Every Day

In-depth daily Bible reading notes for thinking Christians!

Cover to Cover Every Day is constructed on a five-year rolling plan which will take you through the entire Bible, book by book, during that period. In his regular article, 'The Big Picture', Philip Greenslade links the Old and New Testament books in each issue within the wider context of Scripture. Well-known Christian authors and leaders contribute to each issue.

ISSN: 1744-0114
£2.49 each or £13.80 UK annual subscription (6 issues) – from January 2009

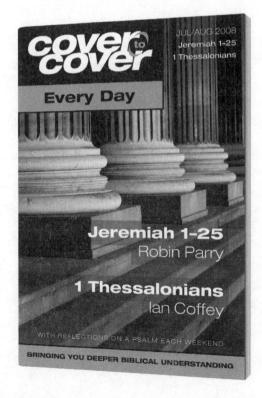

A Passion for God's Story

Discover your place in God's strategic plan! This book is nothing less than the Big Story of 'what on earth God is doing'. Author Philip Greenslade shows how the Bible tells of God's covenants with mankind as part of His redemptive plan, the ultimate goal of which is the new creation.

ISBN: 978-1-84227-094-3
£9.99

Price correct at time of printing